CONSTITUTIONALISM: FOUNDING AND FUTURE

Edited
Kenneth W. Thompson

Volume I
In the Miller Center Bicentennial Series
on Constitutionalism

UNIVERSITY
PRESS OF
AMERICA

The Miller Center

University of Virginia

Copyright © 1989 by

University Press of America,® Inc.

4720 Boston Way
Lanham, MD 20706

3 Henrietta Street
London WC2E 8LU England

British Cataloging in Publication Information Available

Library of Congress Cataloging-in-Publication Data

Constitutionalism : founding and future / edited by Kenneth W.
Thompson.
    p. cm.—(Miller Center bicentennial series on
constitutionalism ; v. 1)
    ISBN 0-8191-7217-9 (alk. paper).   ISBN 0-8191-7218-9 (pbk. : alk.
paper)
    1. United States—Constitutional history.   2. United States—
Politics and government.   I. Thompson, Kenneth W., 1921-   .
II. Series.
JK21.C73 1988
320.973—dc19   88-27707
                                                              CIP

The views expressed by the author(s) of this publication do not necessarily
represent the opinions of the Miller Center. We hold to Jefferson's dictum that:
"Truth is the proper and sufficient antagonist to error, and has nothing
to fear from the conflict, unless by human interposition, disarmed
of her natural weapons, free argument and debate."

Co-published by arrangement with
The White Burkett Miller Center of Public Affairs,
University of Virginia

All University Press of America books are produced on acid-free paper.
The paper used in this publication meets the minimum requirements of American
National Standard for Information Sciences—Permanence of Paper for Printed Library
Materials, ANSI Z39.48-1984.   ∞

TO

JIM, PAM AND COURTNEY

Table of Contents

Preface

The United States of America celebrated the bicentennial of its Constitution in 1987 and in that year the Miller Center of Public Affairs began a series of colloquia on constitutionalism. The aim was to produce a series of papers that would have enduring value in four important areas:

Constitutionalism and the U.S. Constitution

Constitutionalism and the State

The Influence of the U.S. Constitution on the Constitutions of Other Countries

Political Theory and the Constitution

These four areas constitute focal points for the serious discussion of constitutionalism with importance extending beyond the bicentennial. From the time of McIlwain and Beard, the best American thinkers have turned their attention to constitutionalism. It is a subject that provides the cornerstone on which any discussion of democracy can be based. No one can afford to ignore the lessons of constitutionalism as mankind moves into the twenty-first century. Volume I is a living text of such lessons.

Constitutionalism and the administrative state are closely linked. The rule of law is intimately bound up with the organization of governance. The legacy of constitutionalism is not only principles of government but also the working arrangements that make possible the functioning of a political system. Our inclusion of Volume II is based on this premise.

We find it surprising that contemporaries, and especially contemporary presidents, pay so little attention to the historical relationship and mutual interaction of the U.S. Constitution and other constitutions in Asia, Africa, Europe and Latin America. Surely, this was not true at the turn of the century when, in the era of Woodrow Wilson, writers emphasized this relationship. The goal of this series is to help return serious thought and thinkers to a reexamination of what has been called comparative constitutionalism and to provide empirical data that makes this possible.

The U.S. Constitution was written by men who sought not only to fashion a government for themselves but for societies everywhere. They saw their task as creating a political system in which liberty would be preserved not for a day but for all times, not for Americans but all mankind. Lincoln was to address that question nearly a century later and down to the present the question echoes through all the debate over the spread of democracy throughout the world.

The political theorists of the Constitution of 1787 and the Bill of Rights that followed are in truth the Founding Fathers. Their ideas, whether directly or indirectly, found their way into the structure of the Constitution. Some can be considered draftsman of the historic document, which has been called the foremost social invention of all times. (Physical scientists sometimes ask, with a touch of self-righteous arrogance, "To what inventions can social scientists point?") The Constitution may be a more far-reaching invention than the greatest scientific discoveries. At the very least, the theorists played the role that Lord Keynes attributed to intellectuals when he wrote: "Behind every policy choice is the work of some academic scribbler." It is to theorists we turn in seeking to understand the intellectual foundations of public policy.

Introduction

Pundits have commented on what they describe as "overkill" in discussions of constitutionalism in our celebration of the bicentennial. They complain against an outpouring of too many speeches and papers on less and less important points in the Constitution. It is difficult to accept this criticism.

It would be more exact to say that too many political debates are being waged on the basis of half-considered constitutional arguments leading to highly controversial political outcomes. Too often the Constitution becomes a weapon in outright political conflicts. This fact alone would justify the study of constitutionalism and its nature and founding in the United States.

The present volume contains a collection of presentations and essays on basic elements of constitutionalism. They run the gamut from a philosophical inquiry into the distinguishing characteristics of constitutionalism and democracy; an historical analysis of the Virginia Ratification Convention of 1788; an essay on Jefferson and the language of liberty; a critical paper on the presidency in relationship to the constitutional system; and a concluding discussion of the living as distinct from the written constitution.

The philosopher is a rising young scholar whose work bridges law and philosophy and whose interests cluster in the area of applied ethics. Shannon Jordan teaches at George Mason University and is uniquely qualified to address questions of constitutionalism in the context of speech, deeds and the constitution.

Senator William B. Spong, Jr. was a member of the U.S. Senate from Virginia from 1966 to 1973. He has served as dean of the Marshall-Wythe Law School of the College of William and Mary and Dudley Warner Woodbridge Professor of Law. In his essay, he recreates the debate over ratification of the Constitution in the Virginia Convention making it come alive and bringing the personalities into the reader's consciousness as few presentations succeed in doing.

Alf J. Mapp is an eminent historian and literary figure whose book-of-the-month volume, *Thomas Jefferson: A Strange Case of Mistaken Identity* has attracted widespread attention. His discussion of Jefferson's concept of liberty in the framework of constitutionalism gives special meaning to the founding and helps to contrast the Declaration of Independence and the Constitution.

Richard Bolling was for thirty-four years a member of the House of Representatives from the eighty-first to the ninety-sixth Congress. He assesses five American presidents from the standpoint of their understanding and use of the constitutional system. How deep was their comprehension of constitutionalism and to what extent did it provide the guidelines for their actions as president? How did they use or abuse it, understand or misunderstand its significance for a president? Of the five presidents that Congressman Bolling discusses, he ranks President Ford number one for his grasp of the nature of the constitutional system. Several others receive less favorable judgments.

Douglass Cater directs attention to the living constitution and reiterates themes which Shannon Jordan presented in her opening essay. Both Cater and Jordan put stress on "the reactualization" of the Constitution as reinterpreted in the light of changing circumstances. They would agree with Justice Cardozo's phrase that constitutional interpretation involves "filling in the gaps."

No single volume can do more than illuminate the contours of a subject as fundamental as constitutionalism. At most it can call attention to certain neglected aspects of constitutionalism. A philosopher, legal scholar and senator, historian and man of letters, congressman and college president and writer each offer different perspectives of past and present.

Such a group can prepare the way for a discussion of comparative constitutionalism by making clear the essential nature of the U.S. Constitution and the principles and practices that brought it into being. Thus this first volume lays the foundations for other volumes that follow which will analyze the interaction of the U.S. Constitution and the constitutions of Asia, Africa, Europe and Latin America.

Constitutionalism and Democracy

SHANNON JORDAN

NARRATOR: We are pleased to welcome you to a Miller Center lecture by Professor Shannon McIntyre Jordan. Her subject is "Speech, Deeds and the Constitution." Her lecture opens a series specifically addressed to constitutionalism and democracy. The topic is especially appropriate in connection with the bicentennial of the Constitution.

Professor Jordan teaches at George Mason University and received her education at William and Mary and the University of Georgia. She has interests that fall largely in the area of applied ethics, but they also bridge the study of philosophy and law. We feel very privileged to have her with us, and we look forward to the discussion after the presentation.

DR. JORDAN: Thank you. I am very happy to be here. It is an honor to speak again in the Dome Room of the Rotunda and a delight to be back in Charlottesville and at the University.

Another reason that I'm delighted is that the opportunity to speak at a nonprofessional philosopher function allows me to reflect and meditate in a way that is not narrowed by the strict confines of my discipline—which I love and enjoy, but which at the same time has its own boundaries. This lecture allows me to act in a way that is not entirely typical of the philosopher's style, but I think it is important because philosophers need to speak with people in other disciplines.

I would like to present a way of thinking about the word "constitution," which I believe is proper and, more

1

importantly, rewarding for both theoretical and practical political discourse. It is clear that the word "constitution" is both a noun as in the "U.S. Constitution," the written document itself, and a verb meaning to constitute, to build, to found, to set up. In my reflections on the word "constitution," these two senses and the relationship between them will be crucially important. In fact, any meaningful reflection on the concept of constitution must of necessity include reflection upon both speech and deeds.

During the course of this presentation I hope to bring a fresh approach to the concept of political constitution by first seeking to discover its origins in the upsurge of political speech from chaos, and secondly by looking at the relationship between the constitutional document, the text, and the "living constitution," or the contextuality, from within the perspective of hermeneutical philosophy. One implied agenda of the paper is to add to arguments against the view that the Constitution's ultimate meaning is what was in the minds of the framers as well as the objectivist view that the meaning of the Constitution lies solely within the internal structure of the document itself. Finally, I hope these reflections illuminate our thinking about the nature of man and the nature of political existence. In this regard, I will approach the concept of speech, deeds and constitution without any favored assumptions about man's nature, without, for example, the presupposition that since American constitutionalism had at its roots in Locke and other figures, it shares their ideas concerning the nature of man. I will leave the question of human nature open. In other words, one by-product of my reflection should be some insight into the question: What if we first examine the conditions of constitution, the experience of constituting a polity, and then ask what kinds of beings are those who have had such an experience?

Speech and Violence

Supreme Court Justice James Wilson once said, "The people spoke the nation into existence."[1] In this pithy and profound remark we have all the seeds necessary to embark upon a philosophical meditation on the interstices of the three elements of our topic: speech, deeds and constitution.

By reflecting upon the interplay among these three concepts, we will be able to disclose certain aspects of the true meaning of politics, of the fundamental project of the polis, the human city.

My initial hypothesis is that the basis of and the necessity for a polity lies in the fundamental tension between human violence and human speech.[2] This idea has a long and consistent history in political philosophy through philosophers such as Plato, Augustine, Machiavelli, Hobbes and Rousseau. I want to identify that notion, that there is a fundamental tension between human violence and human speech, as a presupposition of the thesis I am developing. My own thesis is that the fundamental act of transcending human violence through speech constitutes a political union. Just as the constitution of the polis springs from and surpasses the chaos of utter individualism, so speech bursts forth and surpasses human violence.

There are, of course, several types of violence which cause human suffering. At one end of the spectrum lies a host of violent events visited upon man by brute force: hurricane, tornado, flood, fire and pestilence have swept down upon peoples and destroyed life, property and tranquility. At the other end of the spectrum lies the ultimate voluntary violence of murder, the senseless slaughter of war and of pathological spree killing. In the middle realm lies the most commonly experienced type of violence, the violence of individual and corporate self-centeredness which is manifested in fear, hatred, and essentially in the desire to dominate the other person, to deprive the other of his self expression, of his will, of his freedom. This self-centeredness, this violence, is clearly manifest in racism, imperialism, and totalitarianism.

Long ago Plato recognized this middle realm of violence in his continued critique of the self-centered rule of the powerful. His dialogues are filled with the drama of the great struggle between, on the one hand, such figures as Thrasymachus in the *Republic*, who champions the idea that political rule both is and should be for the sake of those in power, the rulers, and on the other hand the figure of Socrates, who champions the idea of the reasoned pursuit of truth through speech, which is the foundation of the just polity. It is important to recall that the Sophists who defend the tyrant do so in speech, in the spoken and in the written word, and this remains so, even onto the present day. Those who would deprive the people of their freedom, who would visit upon them the violence of becoming pawns in the ruling party's ideological plans for world domination or utopia, or simply for the satisfaction of the master's whims do so principally through speech. Our century has seen all varieties of this sort of deprivation in fascism, in communism and in economic despotism. The tyrant has his apologists, his party propagandists, for tyranny succeeds far more easily through seduction, persuasion, flattery and cajolery than through brute force. Speech can, therefore, be used in the service of evil or in the service of violence.

It is precisely such observations which point us to the dichotomy between violence and speech. In the Platonic dialogues, once the tyrant's sophistic apologists entered into dialogue with the philosophical Socrates, they were doomed to self contradiction. Once violence, that is the will to dominate others, enters into the realm of speech, it is already a violence attempting to justify itself before the bar of reasoned discourse. To do so, however, is already to begin to negate itself precisely as violence. Paul Ricouer tells us "A person cannot argue for violence without contradicting himself since, by so arguing, he wants to be right and he already enters the field of speech and of discussion leaving his weapon at the door."[3] A being who speaks already engages in the pursuit of a meaning for his experience and meaning always intends, if not universality, at least trans-individuality, trans-particularity. Speaking in its very essence is a sharing between and among people. Speech, as an interpersonal act to intend a shared meaning, already begins to transcend the violence that is born of self-centeredness.

Since the people speaking together transgress radical self-centeredness and initiate the commonwealth, Ricouer observes that "everything political is touched by the turgid play of meaning and violence, for politics exists because the city exists. Therefore, individuals have begun and at least partly succeeded in overcoming their private violence by subordinating it to a rule of law."[4] As Plato's initial and powerful and sustaining metaphor of the *Republic* illustrates, when men engage in dialogue they transcend the chaos of

4

selfish interests and they begin to live in the true polity in speech (*en logoi*). Recall how in the opening scene of the dialogue Socrates is restrained by Polemarchus and the others after he has declined their invitation to remain in the Piraeus with them. They say, "We outnumber you" which is tantamount to saying "We shall force you to stay with us." Socrates' reply is quite simple but astonishing, "Perhaps I can persuade you." Thus begins the long dialogue over the meaning of justice. This isn't just an introduction that Plato wrote to try to get the story started. That metaphor permeates the entire dialogue, it sets the stage and it guides and directs the discourse. Plato is telling us throughout that "justice comes through speech." A great theme of the *Republic* is how the reasoned discourse of Socrates sets a limit upon violence and brings the chaos into an order.

It is helpful here to turn to the ancient Greek meaning for the word "law" as it was used and understood in their culture. The word for law was *nomos* meaning portion, usage, custom, or division. Among possible acts there was a division of usage into those acts which were proper and those which were improper. Custom was that portion of activity deemed proper through usage. Custom divided the social realm into proper segments, each with its allotted roles. The word *nomos* had further roots in *nome,* meaning pasturage, grazing, a spread. Within the pasturage one finds safety, order, and secure identity in the fixed portions. Beyond the pasturage lies the danger of wolves and thieves, and becoming lost in that which is not ordered. The *nome* has boundaries of safety from the threat of chaos and violence. The *nomos* are the walls of the city, the boundaries of safety for a polity where reasoned speech transcends violence and chaos.

The boundaries of the polity emerging from that speech which transcends human violence, thus establishes the meanings of interpersonal relationships within the boundaries, both relationships between persons and relationships between persons and things or property. In this context we can understand why property crimes are violations against the polity itself as well as, of course, violence against the victims. When someone steals my property, it is not so much that he has misappropriated a value, whether it is economic or sentimental, as it is that the theft violates the relationship between him and me. Trust in the common meaning of the language of possession—mine, yours, ours, theirs—is under seige by this deed of theft, as such the deed violates the set boundary, the allotted portions of the polity. He who takes my goods takes little, but he who does so violates me in the sense that he leaves me in chaos. When someone burglarizes my home, I experience the violence of *my* pasturage. I also experience the violation of my polity because my polity, in setting its order and the political boundaries, has agreed that it was *my* home. If man is a political being, then he who harms one citizen does indeed harm all. Thus it is true that if we neglect to cry out against injustices towards any member or any portion of society, we neglect proper stewardship of the polity which we constitute in our speech. This is why it is an ugly hypocrisy for politicians or citizens themselves to speak of "justice" or "the American way" and to simultaneously neglect in their actions the least members of that polity.

I believe that the entire political thrust of the Platonic dialogues can really be summed up in the idea of a reasoned discourse, which brings justice into the world, which brings the order of law, of *nomos*, out of the chaos and thus transcends violence. As Socrates admits in the *Republic*, the true polity, the just state, exists only in speech (*en logoi*).[5] Thus our only real hope is that wise men will contemplate the form of this just polity, thereby constituting their own souls in such a way that they will be able to speak the wisdom which will bring order out of violence and chaos, for the security of law and of the political order is thoroughly rooted in speech.

Speech and Deeds

The objection might be raised, as it is often raised against Plato and anything platonic and against philosophers in general, that philosophers are speaking of the search for political truth. Plato and things platonic, it is suggested, are simply ideals up in the sky not having to do with the real world. It is argued that the philosopher's truth is only in words, that the real world awaits the man of action, a man of deeds.

To answer that objection we must attend to the relationship between speech and deeds as human projects. We have seen that speech constitutes the polity by establishing an order which subdues both violence and chaos and we may, therefore, reasonably conclude that speech itself is a deed. This, of course, is true, but the relationship between speech and deeds is significantly more complex. Hannah Arendt points out that for the ancient Greeks there were shared meanings between human speech and human action.

To understand the nature, the essential meaning of speech and deeds, it is important to look to the product. In fact, Arendt argues that to understand anything, it is important to look to the product of the activity in question. "Distinguished from both consumer goods and use objects, there are finally the products of action and speech which together constitute the fabric of human relationships and affairs."[6]

To understand the meaning of writing a poem or building a home or planting a garden, one must look to the product of the activity: the completed poem, the lived-in home, the harvest and consumption of the food. This is obvious on the level of these examples, but Arendt claims that this is likewise true for human speech and human action, and that these both aim at the construction, modification, reenactment or fabrication of human relationships. In other words, human speech and human action aim at the political and they are essentially political. They are political by nature. It is important, I think, to add to this observation that even the so-called "productive" sciences, even building and farming, have an essentially political dimension. For Aristotle it is for this reason that politics is the architectonic of all the disciplines in the practical domain. For Aristotle, all human activity is essentially political and must therefore be guided by the principles which direct and guide politics. No matter what we do, our actions as persons enter into the political domain. This line of thought indicates why the discipline of economics is *best* understood not as an independent mathematically modelled science, but as that branch of moral philosophy called political economy. Moreover, the realm of human actions which do not in some way have political meanings in the sense of affecting the fabric of human relationships must be considered to be quite small. Recent scholarship in the human sciences has certainly disclosed the social content of even the seemingly smallest human action.[7] It seems obvious that human actions which have their Telos in products of a material nature, for example, engineering, or other activities characterized as *techne*, are easily seen as actions with political consequences, overtones and meanings. Strictly speaking, however, Arendt's definition stands: those actions which have the *specific telos* and the specific purpose of constituting, modifying and affecting human relationships, are political deeds in the fullest sense of that word. Of course, Arendt says that these deeds are the "products of action and speech,"[8] and this leads us to the important idea of the interweaving of speech and deeds for discussion of all political matters.

Just as the very meaning of human actions and deeds arises as they are spoken of, the very content of all speech about the polity also has human action as its meaning, as its intention or its content. This interdependence of speech and deeds has been observed by the political theorist Bruce Smith who says that "public speech most often depends upon deeds for its subject matter, but the deed (the unique action) depends upon speech for its power. Nothing is more fleeting than the deed. Only through speech can the deed remain entire and intact, distinguishable from and undissolved by the multitude of its consequences."[9]

Whether as political rhetoric in the practical realm, or as theoretical discourses of political science or political philosophy, public speech talks about human action, human deeds. In fact, human custom is that which calls into existence both political philosophy and practical politics. *As soon as* political discourse of any kind happens, it is already a testimony to speech articulating or trying to articulate the meaning of the deeds. Conversely, as Smith's observation puts it, the *power* of the deed itself lies in its being spoken of; only in becoming part of the political discourse, and becoming part of the tradition of the people's heritage of values, does the deed have the power to endure across time. Thus, while at first glance, deeds may be seen as occurring in time prior to speech, the very meaning of the deed lies precisely in its becoming the content of some future speech.

From another perspective, shall we say a logical or ontological perspective, speech is prior to deeds. Moreover, for all but the most original political activity—that is, the original political genius which launches a tradition within a political discourse[10]—deeds occur within already fabricated social contexts within an existing polity. When we engage in human actions, we do so within an array of possible deeds already on hand by the preunderstood meaning of deeds as they are spoken of in our speech. A doer of deeds preunderstands the meaning of human action *prior to* his acting precisely because the political discourse of a potential actor has already constituted the polity, the human arena in which the action will take place. Although it is a topic for discussion beyond the scope of this paper, I think it is helpful to note here that cross-cultural misunderstandings, as they often occur in the international political arena or in the interethnic political factiousness of the polyglot polity, often arise because of differing preunderstandings about the meaning of deeds. The deeds appear to be the same, but the point here is that they are in fact not the same; they arise within different contexts and therefore carry different meanings.

The acting and speaking together of a people constitutes the relations among people, which is to say the acting and speaking constitutes the polity. The state is not properly understood as a physical location, i.e., this sea to shining sea, these amber waves of grain, or even of these alabaster cities undimmed by human tears. That is not the nation. That is not the polity. The polity is more precisely that way of being, that organization of human relationships which arises from the way the people speak and act together. This is why William F. Harris, writing on American Constitutionalism says: "The words narrate the polity into existence, and as its working principles unfold the polity becomes a kind of large scale text in its own right."[11]

I will return to this notion of the polity as text in its own right in the following section, but first I believe it is necessary to further explore Ricouer's notion that the polity is brushed with the interplay of violence and speech by attending to the concept of political power. When a people come together in speech and deed, they constitute the space in which human relationships become lived for a specific purpose, i.e., the way in which a people speak their polity into existence constitutes the polity in its particular individual characteristics. The form that a polity takes in its constitution inclines the citizens toward specific, actual ways of being, acting and relating toward certain deeds from amongst all the potential ways persons could be, act, etc. The constitution of a polity, then, is the initial instance of political power. It creates the unique power-to-be for human beings who will live out their potentialities within the political realm. Hannah Arendt, again, offers us an insight:

> Power springs up between men when they act together and it vanishes the moment they disperse. Because of this peculiarity, which power shares with all potentialities that can only be actualized but never fully materialized, the only indispensable material factor in the generation of power is the living together of people. Only where men live so close together that the potentialities of action are always present can power remain present. . . And whoever, for whatever reason, isolates himself and does not partake in this being together forfeits power and becomes impotent no matter how great and valid his reasons.[12]

Because political power is precisely nothing other than the potentiality of persons who are speaking and acting together, power must be understood as different from political force. The tyrant may exert force, but political power continues to reside with the way the peoples speak their polity into existence. If the force of the tyrant is brute violence, or the threat of it, the people may, out of fear, fall silent, in which case political power in its fundamental sense falls out of existence for their polity. It might even be said that the polity itself disappears and that the brute organization of human doings that is administered by sheer force is all that remains, in which case violence has silenced speech.

As we have seen, however, tyrants prefer and usually are able to rule by persuasion and flattery. This observation leads us to face the most insidious violence of all. When the leader persuades the people, or when a people allow themselves to marshall their energies—all too often under the guise of some transcending principle like "law and order" or "protection of the fatherland," or "for the sake of the revolution and the new order"—into a political force which forgets the dichotomy between speech and violence, the people lose political power. When a people, at least partially, overcome their private violence by subordinating the greed, envy and animosity of self-centeredness in their speaking together, the constitution of their polity becomes a reality. The political power of the polity remains, however, only as long as their speaking transcends the violence of their disconnected private desires. When a people speak their polity into the text of a legal code, the laws are expressive of the "will of the people," and the rule of law is superordinate to private will. If a people do not attend to the speech which constitutes the polity which transcends violence, then even the rule of law can manifest the violence of fear, distrust, wounded pride or the will to dominate others. As Ricouer tells us, "Thus, the rule of law which gives form to the social body is also (at least potentially) a political force, an enormous violence which elbows its way through our private violences and speaks the language of value and honor."[13] We can recognize this violence in the divisive rhetoric of extreme chauvinists, of racist demagogues, of narrow sectarians, and of apologists for various moral principles. Political power, however, is grounded in the unity of persons which is effected through and expressed in political speech and action, that speech and action which transcends the divisiveness of violence and chaos, which aims at the establishment and maintenance of human relationships.

Constitution as Founding Discourse

In order to illuminate more completely the relationship between speech and deeds we must now turn to the third element of our discussion: constitution. The original speaking into existence of a polis may be seen through historiography as a people's response to those circumstances which do violence to their lives. For example, when the Founding Fathers bespoke the American colonies into a nation, a unique polity, they specifically addressed grievances against the British government. Once spoken into existence, however, the polity must continue to bespeak an order into existence out of the chaos and violence which threatens every generation of individuals. Bernard Dauenhauer expresses this very point. For him, "the founding discourse must fit the founding community and the circumstances to which it is addressed if it is to acquire an authority. Once the founding discourse is accepted as founding, then subsequent discourse will be measured against it."[14] Political philosophy thus says that when the new polity bursts forth onto the stage of human history, its authority must become a heritage of value with sufficient political power to become a tradition for future generations, otherwise the polity will have no history.

How is it possible, though, for a founding discourse, which speaks the deeds of the founding fathers into a polity, to retain its authority down through the ages? The answer is surprisingly simple and yet it is deceptively complex. In a word, the answer is *language*. It has been observed that language is a body of signs, words, that are held together by a common code called grammar. If this be so, then lexicography and the logic of grammar constitute a philosophy of language, but my colleagues tell me this is decidedly not true. Such a reduction of the problem of language leaves out what Ricouer and other hermeneutical philosophers call the diachronic character of language.

Although they are in dictionaries, words are "only available signs delimited by other signs within the same system by the common code. These signs become words charged with expression and meaning when they come to fruition in a sentence, when they are used. . . . They have

real meaning only in that passing instance of discourse that
we call a sentence."[15] The point here is that the event of
speaking, the utterance, gives life to language and charges
words with meaning.

So, as previously mentioned, language permits the
founding discourse—the speaking into existence of a political
union—to become an authority of tradition. Of course, the
constitution of a polity by founding discourse becomes the
ultimate law of the people. It is the Constitution as the
written document, as the written word, as the text, which
preserves for tradition the constituting speech of the
founders. This written text, then, assumes supreme political
value for the heritage that it is nurturing. As Ricouer
observes in another context, "Language . . . is fixed
through writing. Transmission of heritage is thereby
assured to the documents . . . because it is offered to the
interpretation of the following generations."[16]

The fixing of the founding discourse, the originating
political speech, by the written text renders the authority
of tradition a far greater political value than the mere oral
tradition of values. Once the written document fixes the
founding discourse it perdures as a kind of "sacred witness"
through the ages. Note, for example, the almost tabernacle
housing in the National Archives of the original parchment
of the American Declaration of Independence and the
Constitution. After taking hold on a people, tradition and
its textual witness transmit the "authority of the
past . . . Tradition is not limited to describing our
dependence on the past as fact, instead it accords a positive
value to that dependence. It presumes the superiority of
certain teaching because it is old, or ancient or even
archaic."[17] Tradition is the possibility that future
generations have for taking the founding discourse and
making it their own.

Does, however, the elevation of the founding political
discourse into law create an oppressive rule by and from the
past? Many philosophers worry over that question. Indeed,
there are those who would declare that the truth of the
Constitution lies nowhere but in the intentions of its
authors. However, to claim that what is in the mind of the
framers is the ultimate rule, is the final authority for
political discourse, would be to make false idols of

temporally finite speakers who, however prescient and wise, remain only finitely human. After all the founding fathers, the framers, spoke out of their specific historical context in response to specific problems or threats of human violence. To reify the minds of the framers denies the validity and the very meaning of tradition as the heritage of authoritative values. We are brought then by our reflections to a consideration of the relationship between Constitution as text and the continual constitution of the polity in political speech, that is, to the authority of the past and its interpretation in the present. This in turn, will force us to confront the essential temporality of human existence.

Speaking specifically of the Constitution itself, Harris wrote that, "once written, a work leaves the control of its writer. Words of the Constitution, once they began bringing a polity into force, lost their bond with the thoughts of the framers and established a bond with the political order."[18] The meaning of the language of the Constitution cannot then reside in the text or the document as though meaning were an external object, anymore than it can reside in the minds of the authors. The meaning of the Constitutional document, rather, arises in the relationship between the text and the people who accept its authority in their continual reinterpretation of it.[19] Constitutional history then can be understood as a dialogue between generations, even between ages.

By suspending the ephemeral quality of speech, language, when embedded in the text, lifts the meaning of speech out of its sociohistorical conditioning; the founding discourse is thus free to become valuable beyond the immediate circumstances provoking it. Further, as Ricouer observed, "in freeing itself with regard to its initial audience . . . the text is open to a whole series of reinterpretations which reactualize it each time in a new situation."[20] We need to attend closely to the last phrase "reinterpretations which reactualize it each time in a new situation." In language-as-text, the constitutional document frees the founding political discourse, that speech which in subduing violence initiates a political power with sufficient authority to become a heritage of values that will endure across time. This Constitutional document expresses the polity by providing its written boundaries, insofar as it describes the ultimate law of and for the people. This speech, freed by the text we know as the Constitution, defines the boundary between violence and political life. Again, Dauenhauer expresses it nicely: "not to keep one's utterances under the aegis of the discourse of the Founding Fathers is to revolt. To place one's utterances under the aegis of the political discourse of aliens is to commit treason."[21] Revolution and treason are high crimes because they are the ultimate political violence. They pit themselves against the very speech which the people hold as that political power which protects them from the violence surrounding their borders. Revolution and treason are deconstituting acts. These notions point to an entire region of political philosophy just beyond the confines of this paper; these are the topics of revolution and civil disobedience and when and how they are justified and how they differ from criminal disobedience of the law. We have found here, however, that political speech arises within the context of a living people and finds its meaning in the relationships between the people and their originating or founding discourse which is now present in a textual document and is open to living reinterpretations to maintain its relevance, to make the tradition alive for the people.

Jefferson told us that every generation should come together and write its own constitution. In fact, they do, otherwise freedom has no meaning. We do not, of course, sit down and rewrite the original document at a constitutional convention, but constitution is an ongoing process. In grammatical terms it is quite simply a verb as well as noun. To be sure, the written text holds a privileged position in political discourse inasmuch as the ultimate political deed is the constitution of the polity, speaking the polity into existence. Political speech is, however, both reflective of and constitutive of the political order; it both reveals and constitutes. True political speech is set firmly within the confines of the founding discourse and it meaningfully addresses the living situation of a people in the present as it constitutes them anew as a polity by directing their vision into the future.

Speech, Deeds and Constitution

It remains then for us to look at the temporal dimensions of the political realm in order to finally understand the ground of this triptych of a polis: speech, deeds and constitution. We have seen that the Constitution-as-text lifts the founding discourse out of its original historical context. This freeing of the founding discourse permits it to become authoritative speech for a whole tradition. We have also noted the necessity for this tradition to renew, to reinterpret and to reactualize the authority of the written text for succeeding historical contexts. Finally, we have seen that the very essence of language renders possible the freeing of speech into text (writing) and the release of the text meaning by further speech (interpretation of writing): the essence of language then is to be both synchronic, that is, captured within the time, and diachronic, moving across the time. The grammar and signs of language gather up the meaning of speech into a synchronic whole. Speech, however, both original speech and the interpretation of the text, is diachronic: speaking or uttering sentences into meaningful expressions occurs across time.

We have been led by our reflections to confirm a particular view of human being and its political existence, a view that has a history deep in the roots of western philosophy: that man is a thoroughly finite creature and that his polity is therefore of necessity a tenuous order. Consequently, the genius of American constitutionalism lies in its open-mindedness, its constant recognition of its own fleeting hold on the affairs of man, its need to renew itself. If the text and the context correlation of the meaning of constitution confirms anything, it is that the speech and deeds of a people do in fact constitute their polity. The polity that a people speak into being is their own very tenuous hold on an order threatened by violence which lies just beyond the borders of their spirit. The birth of a polity in that speech which overcomes violence, always requiring rebirth or renewal, is a constantly humbling experience. If we were to seek a conclusion from these reflections, perhaps it is best expressed in this reminder: finite man must be ever humble in his politics.

Consider again Justice Wilson's interpretation of the Constitution in his utterance (now fixed in writing) that "the people spoke the United States into existence." The founding discourse originally is diachronic. The patriotic speeches, declarations, debates, even leaders rallying the crowds of the militia, comprise that speech with which the people draw boundaries against the violences of their context, in the American case the transgressions of the British. These speeches, however, become fixed in such documents as the Declaration, the Constitution, the Federalist Papers, and the Bill of Rights. Thus freed into the synchronic language of the text, a past context is portended into a context for the future. When we interpret the past as fixed before us in our present by the written text of the Constitution, we project into our future a meaningful context in which our deeds will be safe within the boundaries of our political discourse. In retrieving the past by reinterpreting the text, we renew the meaning of that speech from the past and we move forward into the future. In the political activity of interpreting the written Constitution, we are extending our laws, the nomos, we are pushing the boundaries of our pasturage into the present, and hopefully into the future. In short, we are constituting our present political realm by reconstituting our original discourse, the founding discourse of our polity.

In learning the profound role of political speech in founding and preserving, that is to say in constituting a polity, we are led to a two-fold project for further reflection. One is rather theoretical and the other is somewhat more practical. In concluding this paper I wish to indicate these directions for further reflection and even research to bring the unsaid of this present into the future.

First, concerning the more theoretical reflections on the place of a consideration of language in philosophical discourse on politics, I think the entire question of meaning of language must be addressed. Clearly, the notion of meaning is integral to any notion of reason or rational discourse which we employ when pitting the power of speech against the forces of violence. Thus, just as reason or rationality cannot be reduced to logical structure or instrumentality, the topic of meaning cannot be truly exhausted by an analysis of the internal set of rules employed in a single universe of discourse. The meaning of meaning, I suggest, will be as pluralistic as a true and just polity, but this does not render the notion of meaning any more senseless or antirational than the notion of pluralistic values renders a society chaotic and without unity. In fact, I would venture to suggest that even the most theoretical discussion of language, of meaning, of speech, of reason by philosophy can profit enormously if it is nurtured by the ground of everyday practical experiences, especially of political existence. Finally, just as a tradition informs the community through a specific heritage of values across time, the meaning of speech also unfolds across the history of a discourse which creates the boundaries within which a topic can be discussed. Consequently, the meaning, the logic and the standards of rationality for any discourse emerge from the initiating experience for that speech. The meaning of any speech, therefore, is both its origin and its goal. The phenomenon or experience springs forth into speech and as such is the goal of that speech.

With regard to the practical dimensions of my reflections on speech, deeds and constitution, I wish to suggest two specific topics for further reflection and make a final cautionary remark. First, the fundamental tension between speech and human violence must remain a guiding truth even when on a practical level the polity necessarily resorts to a kind of violence in order to preserve its very integrity. The examples of war and political revolution illustrate the point. As long as people recognize the fundamental opposition of speech and violence they can prevent the self-delusion that they have that they can completely supersede all human violence. For example, the rhetoric of "the war to end all wars" or "revolution for the establishment of utopia" or "the thousand year Reich" is blatantly seen to be false language. On the other side, as long as we continue to recognize the opposition of political discourse in human violence, then, should we resort out of terrible necessities to the violence of war or revolution, we would recognize our own culpability, our own failure, our own limited perspective. On this point, Ricouer observes that "he who calls a crime a crime is already on the road to meaning because he speaks and he is on the road to salvation because he is transcending the violence that he commits."[22] The practical ramifications for either war or revolution here would be that even as we engage in violent deeds, we recognize the other side as persons capable of speech, hence of reasoned dialogue which can resolve differences. Even an extreme case such as regicide, as in the case of the Lutheran Minister, Dietrich Bonhoeffer's plot to kill Hitler, will, however rational, be recognized as murder. (How else can the Christian minister contemplate the deed?)

A second point is the role of nonviolent political protest which I believe should be examined given our current political situation. The act of civil disobedience, whether we speak of Ghandi, Martin Luther King, or the contemporary Sanctuary Movement (although they themselves say they are not engaged in civil disobedience) should be considered at least in part as the act of witnessing the nonviolent aspirations of political speech, the nonviolent aspirations of the society itself. Civil disobedience can be understood as a testimony to the very foundations of the polity in its origin and goal.

Finally, a word of caution: in all discourse, whether explicitly political discourse or a supposed separate theoretical science, a kind of humility must always permeate speech. This is necessary because the tension between speech and violence is a fundamental trait of human existence. Violence always surrounds the boundaries of speech, and as such, it is an ever present danger. Indeed, violence threatens speech for it can, as we have already seen, insinuate itself into the very heart of any discourse. Once again Paul Ricouer nicely makes the point, "Violence in discourse consists in the claim that a single one of its modalities exhausts the realm of speech. To be nonviolent in discourse is to respect the plurality and diversity of language."[23]

It is a matter of profound political consequence that we bear this caution in mind at both the practical and theoretical level of discourse, for these two are inseparable for the political existence of human beings. Practically, we must respect the plurality of traditions in forming the pluralistic moral communities of humanity. Theoretically, we must learn to allow the various modes of discourse to remain in their proper spheres: let each natural science or human science grow so long as it remains true to the phenomenon which gave birth to it; let each language of calculation remain a productive science with its proper place in the architectonic of political discourse; let the prophetic speech of myth and the metaphors of profound symbolic narrative disclose for us the heart of man, of the universe, and insofar as it becomes unhidden, of the divine. Respecting the uniqueness of the relations between and the multiplicity of the varieties of human discourse provides us with respect for mankind in all its plurality. Ultimately such respect may very well be the key to rational meaning, to reasoned inquiry, to speech overcoming violence, and to the city of man constituting a true and just polity. Thank you.

QUESTION: Where do nonverbal interchange and nonverbal communication fit into your scheme?

DR. JORDAN: I think that it's possible to say that deeds or actions are nonverbal communications. It is also possible to say that certain actions are a kind of speech. Part of Arendt's point was that we can't really make a break between speech and action, so when people are communicating, whether through deeds or speech, they are establishing human relationships. She wants us to look at the unity that comes from the action and the speech because the ultimate goal is the same.

COMMENT: Although I don't mean to pursue the topic here, I do want to mention that your talk is completely counter to some of the new developments in anthropology concerning nonverbal behavior and the distinction between speech and symbolic meaning. Even though I don't necessarily agree with these views, I believe that your topic needs to consider the nonverbal, nonsymbolic aspects of human communication.

DR. JORDAN: What do you mean by "nonsymbolic?"

COMMENT: In speech, most of the meaning of language is symbolic. I'm talking about the nonsymbolic aspects of communication, such as distinguishing between violent and nonviolent speech. The main way to make a distinction is through the nonsymbolic behavioral aspect. This is a huge topic. I thought I would bring this up for consideration for the future.

DR. JORDAN: I appreciate that. I think that I'm aware of what you are saying, and I will work from Arendt's perspective in order to respond to that. If I understand your assertion correctly, the area of scholarship that you are pointing to involves the idea that the meaning of an action in the world is not necessarily conveyed by the action itself. For example, an action, such as someone giving me flowers is not necessarily conveyed by receiving the flowers and then having the flowers. One needs also to know who is giving me the flowers and why they are giving me the flowers. I am able to know not from what is said or from the action of giving the flowers, because the action itself, if simply contained in its immediate description, could be the action of a lover or an enemy. Is this what you are pointing to? Other contexts allow me to know the meaning of that action. So I know, "Ah, he is giving me the flowers because he is mad at me and he wants me to go home and fix his dinner;" or, "He is giving me the flowers because he loves me and he is saying he loves me today." I figure that out not from what is said or specifically what is done but from knowing a whole history and context with which to make my judgment and interpretation of the action.

I think the import that has for this presentation is that history allows us to interpret, reflect, consider or analyze the meaning of a specific speech or action. I cannot make sense simply out of the words that are given but the words themselves have a whole history. My experience with a person has a whole history and my experience of the nation has a whole history. When I make my judgments, I bring all that to bear in my interpretation of the meaning of what is happening. I'm not sure I see how that would in any way jeopardize what I've presented here, but I will think about it some more.

QUESTION: If we look at the writings of John Locke, we see that he justified the violence in the English revolution of 1688. Thomas Jefferson's writings also justify violence under certain circumstances. This is also the case of Martin Luther. Their writings and speeches can be judged as a justified end result that leads to violence of a sort. In those three cases, I think they were certainly justified. Is there a measure of relativity in this sort of thing? The writings are glorious in retrospect, but in a sense they all legitimated the resort to violence.

DR. JORDAN: What you say is true. No speaker has complete control over the meaning of his words. As speakers, we like to think that we do, but in fact we don't. We see that most dramatically when we try to speak with people whom we don't know very well. We can be using the same word in the same sentence, but it can have different meaning than we intend. Obviously there is a whole body of scholarship on this subject, but the act of speaking is an interpersonal act.

I will use Luther's case to prove some of my points. If his words were interpreted differently, and we were close in time, I would say to him, "Think again; speak it again and see if your form is correct; look at the possible consequences." He didn't want to start a reformation, yet he did want to reform, and that kind of reforming was only possible with the type of violence that actually occurred. Thus, he certainly is in part responsible for that. I wouldn't say that he bears full moral responsibility for everything that happened, such as all the religious wars, but his speaking certainly initiated it. As the people took it up, his speech gained its full meaning. So the Ninety-nine Theses have a meaning to Lutherans that is entirely different than the meaning it has for Catholics.

QUESTION: I'm not at all sure this is an appropriate question to ask, but your opinion would be very helpful to me. How does a philosopher look at Proposition 63 that was put up for referendum? I don't know its full content, but it is related to the idea of compulsory education in English in California schools.

DR. JORDAN: Even though we may not know the precise content of the proposal, I can give my response to the idea that the English language should be the language of the schools and that the children must learn it when they go to school.

There are two tidy ways of coming at that, but I find neither one of them very satisfactory. On the one hand, the child's prospects for the future are severely damaged in this country if he is not completely fluent in the English language. Since the purpose of the schools is at least in part to prepare the child to live in the U.S. and to be a citizen, the child needs the English language. On the other side, it seems to me that one of the sadnesses of being a melting pot is that we become sort of bland. Everything is put together into the pot and there isn't anything really identifiable, but you drink it and call it "soup." I think that people really need their traditions and their heritages.

Although I'm not familiar with this, I wonder if the very heavy influx of Southeast Asians in the last few years may have induced this proposition. Southeast Asians did not come voluntarily and they were not ready. They were not like the Irishman who said "I already speak the language so I'm going to go over there and make my fortune and send for my sisters, brothers, aunts, uncles, and cousins." They came out of political necessity and tragedy. Therefore, their coming doesn't have the same kind of meaning. Consequently, they cannot be understood or responded to in the same way as the coming of the European immigrant.

Once a child goes to school and is exposed to the language of the newspaper, the movie theaters and the rock music, the child becomes an English-speaking person. Taking the language away implies taking the culture away, and I find that very frightening. So if it were mine to do, I would have a Solomonic response and say, "I'm going to let you decide." In other words, let the people decide for themselves what they want to do about that particular issue because it is integral to their self understanding. Thus, the state ought not to make an immediate decision—the state will have practical problems since teachers in different languages will have to be trained—simply because it provides the compulsory education. Even though there is this practical problem, it seems to me the state ought not to violate the integrity of those peoples if they choose not to do so.

QUESTION: On the one hand, it seems like the state is making a decision for them, but on the other hand, the state may want to guard against some divisive things. Also, the state might see that this is a way to really integrate the nation and maintain unity. Does philosophy play a role in the process somewhere along the line as we make a decision to go one way or the other?

DR. JORDAN: Yes, I think that on both sides there is moral political reasoning; that is, we are talking about the values that people hold, how to respect persons and what is the best thing to do in the sense of good or right. I think that people could probably legitimately argue for either conclusion. When I get into that kind of a bind, I find that I'm most comfortable opting for respect for individuals and making sure that they are very well informed about the decision and choices they are making. If you choose to raise your child in a language other than English in California, you are doing certain kinds of things to that child and his future.

The situation is similar to the one parents face when they decide to raise their child as a Catholic, a Methodist or a Buddhist. Parents opt for something about that child's future and, although the child does not decide, the child lives with it forever. He may change; he may grow up and learn English, but that's not the same thing as being raised with English as the first language. Likewise, he may grow up and reject any and all religions, but that's not the same thing as growing up without a religion. In those kinds of situations I think that the morally preferable option is to inform the people carefully about the choices they are making. They should also be informed about the anticipated consequences. Once this is done, they should be allowed to make the decisions unless there is some overriding political reason.

QUESTION: You've spoken mostly about how speech can act as a brake or a protection against violence, but not so much about the other direction, in which speech can be an incitement to violence. I wonder to what extent these two directions come into tension. Would you comment on this issue?

DR. JORDAN: We will always face the fact that pacifism and non-violence is beautiful. Yet, I confess that I have not been able to live my life without violence. My life has not been exempt from minimal kinds of violence. Although nobody has even ever thought about having me arrested, I have faced situations that involve violent speech which is destructive throughout my life.

QUESTION: Are you talking about violent speech as a violent deed?

DR. JORDAN: Yes, when speech is violent, it constitutes a violent deed, and that's destructive. Plato would argue that violent speech is not true speech. Christian language holds, "I am fallen when I speak violently." Sometimes, it seems to me, as I indicated in the paper, it is necessary to declare "I am not a pacifist," although pacifists would argue against this. I think that sometimes it is necessary to use violence. If we do that with tremendous humility and care, it is my hope that we will still try to speak truly through the use of that violence.

For example, when we train young men to go off and fight in war, one of the things that we ought not do is train them to undertake the violence that is necessary in war by dehumanizing the enemy or by using profane or derogative names such as "gook." You shouldn't train them to punch bayonets into bags and say at the same time, "this is for you, gook," because then they are dehumanizing the enemy and therefore destroying the truth of the violence.

I firmly believe that fighting for justice is a possibility. I don't think, however, that is the first line. I think there are all kinds of other things we need to do before we start fighting for justice. We can strive for justice in other ways, but we may have to do violence in order to achieve justice. Policemen do it every day and I'm certainly not in favor of disarming the police. For the same reasons, I'm not in favor of disarming the country. Given that, what are my constraints if I'm acting violently?

An anecdote will help me here. My father was a military man and I remember that the first time I asked him what a war crime was, he said, "A war crime is something that your enemy does in the name of justice or goodness that makes it impossible for you to shake his hand after you have defeated him. A war crime makes it impossible for you to look him in the eye after you have defeated him." I was much too young for this definition, but I remember him saying those words, and then I began trying to find out what they meant. He meant that you can kill a man, but you can't rape his wife. You can kill a man, but you can't torture him. My father was after the good notion that we must still remain true in our speaking and in our understandings even though we are committing a violent act. On the other side there is a problem about inciting to violence for an evil purpose. Plato would define that as sophistic speech or as speech that is not true, as in a case where I try to incite people to revolution that is unjustified.

QUESTION: I have problems with your analogy of the good war, and the notion that in the war there are some individuals who are blocked from carrying out good violence and don't shoot their guns or miss on purpose, while there are others who are encouraged by the war to come home and carry on violence in other than noble causes. In general terms, your analysis of the relationship of deed and speech and on the means to control evil and violence is based on what is morally correct, rather than on how people actually behave, whether or not they are motivated to control evil and to eliminate violence.

DR. JORDAN: Right, I have not done a sociological analysis of what people in fact do. I have been talking about what people ought to do and that's an entirely different level, though I would say that it's not unrelated. Let me take the example of the individual who comes back from the war and enters into a life of crime. Why did that happen? I do not think that that phenomenon is unrelated to Lt. Calley's defense plea that he was not guilty. Calley admitted that he had shot the people dead, but he argued that was he not guilty of murder because he had killed the enemy. He said that the enemy was "nameless, ageless, sexless, and faceless." In other words he had totally dehumanized those people. He felt that he wasn't killing women, children, old men, and unarmed people, but "enemies." When you can dehumanize the Vietnamese, you can come home and dehumanize the people who live around the corner. It's no different. You are dehumanizing human beings.

Thus, it is important to consider how we ought to speak. We should try to form speech which will inform our deeds and move us to seek a political union which establishes relationships that are not violent. In this scheme, the ultimate violence is to overcome your will in my interest. Unfortunately, that happens in business, politics and in all kinds of human relations, including the family. If we try to speak truly, speech will always, as Ricouer says, "try to maintain the interpersonal" because the meaning will be in the relatedness and in the relationship, not in "what I said it was" or "how you want to hear it." The meaning is in how we can get together and transcend the isolation which spawns violence.

NARRATOR: Well, we certainly want to think continuously about this kind of issue. For those of you who had questions, one of your tributes was that you made it very clear that you had been prompted to think about these issues. Professor Jordan has spoken of a great tradition, the natural law and the natural rights tradition. We couldn't have had a better source of inspiration than Professor Jordan's lecture. We thank her very much.

ENDNOTES

1. *Chisholm v. Georgia*, 2 DA11. 419 (1793).

2. Further discussion of this topic lies beyond the range of this paper, but I identify it as a presupposition of the thesis I am developing. It is my contention, along with many contemporary philosophers, that there can be no presuppositionless philosophy, thus the honest identification of the presuppositions of one's work is not merely helpful but intellectually required.

3. Paul Ricouer, *Political and Social Essays*, (Athens: Ohio University Press, 1974), p. 90.

4. *Ibid.*, pp. 93-94.

5. Alan Bloom, *The Republic of Plato*, (New York: Basic Books, Inc., 1968), p. 274, 592 ab.

6. Hannah Arendt, *The Human Condition*, (Chicago: University of Chicago Press, 1958), p. 94.

7. See, for example, Irving Goffman, *Relations in Public*, (New York: Harper and Row, 1971), and Alfred Schutz, *The Phenomenology of the Social World*, (Evanston: Northwestern University Press, 1967).

8. Arendt, *op. cit.*, p. 94.

9. Bruce James Smith, *Politics and Remembrance*, (Princeton: Princeton University Press, 1985), p. 119.

10. The whole question of political genius, vi 2., one whose speeches and deeds re-articulate a vision of human order, turns on the genius as *outside* the polity even as he is historically in it. Although this issue lies beyond the scope of this paper, I would argue that the famous allegory of the cave in Plato's *Republic* is an

28

expression of the dilemma of political genius. More recently, though in the context of cultural anthropology, Kenelm Burridge makes a similar point about culture and the extra- or trans-cultural self. *Someone, No One: An Essay on Individuality*, (Princeton: Princeton University Press, 1979).

11. William F. Harris II, "Bonding Word and Polity: The Logic of American Constitutionalism," *The American Political Science Review*, Vol. 76, p. 34.

12. Arendt, *op. cit.*, pp. 200-201.

13. Ricouer, *op. cit.*, p. 94.

14. Bernard P. Dauenhauer, *Silence: The Phenomenon and Its Ontological Significance*, (Bloomington: Indiana University Press, 1980), pp. 38-39.

15. Ricouer, *op. cit.*, p. 92.

16. *Ibid.*, p. 246.

17. *Ibid.*

18. Harris, *op. cit.*, p. 44.

19. *Ibid.*, p. 35.

20. Ricouer, *op. cit.*, p. 260.

21. Dauenhauer, *op. cit.*, p. 40.

22. Ricouer, *op. cit.*, p. 100.

23. *Ibid.*, p. 101.

The Virginia Ratification Convention of 1788

SENATOR WILLIAM B. SPONG, JR.

NARRATOR: It is a pleasure to welcome Senator Spong, whose topic is the U.S. Constitution and Virginia's ratification of it.

Senator Spong represented Virginia in the U.S. Senate from 1966 to 1973. He received formal education at Hampden Sydney College and the University of Virginia Law School. In addition, he is the recipient of honorary degrees from Hampden Sydney, Washington and Lee, the College of William and Mary, and Roanoke College. Appropriately, given his subject, he served in the Virginia House of Delegates from 1954 to 1955, and the Virginia State Senate from 1956 to 1966. In the wider area of public service, he has been chairman of the Virginia Commission on Public Education, chairman of the Commission on Virginia's Future, president of the Virginia Bar Association, and trustee of the Virginia State Library. His allegiance as teacher and scholar has been to the College of William and Mary beginning in 1948 as Lecturer, then Cutler Lecturer, then Dudley Warner Woodbridge Professor of Law at the Marshall-Wythe Law School and thereafter dean of that institution. He has taught and done research at a number of other educational institutions including the University of London, the Salzburg Seminar, the Woodrow Wilson Center at the Smithsonian, and the University of Virginia Law School, where he served as Ewald Distinguished Professor of Law.

It's a great pleasure and privilege to have someone who cares as much about this state as Senator Spong with us today to speak on the Virginia ratification process with special reference to the presidency.

SENATOR SPONG: Thank you, Ken, for that gracious introduction. As you have indicated, I am going to speak very generally about the Virginia Ratification Convention of 1788. It is a timely topic because in our observance of the bicentennial of the Constitution we are now in the midst of the ratification process. At this time 200 years ago the Constitution had been approved in Philadelphia and the various states were meeting to ratify it. It is interesting that the people in Philadelphia, who were very wise, did not trust the fate of the Constitution to the state legislatures. In Virginia it would not have met with a warm reception. Instead they suggested that special conventions be convened in each of the states for the purpose of rejecting or adopting a new Constitution. It is such a convention in Virginia that I will discuss.

Aside from its timeliness, I think the Virginia ratification debates should be regarded as among the most masterful political discourses that have occurred in the English-speaking world. Also, the Convention may have been the best-run political operation that has ever taken place in the United States.

Two hundred years ago, Virginia reached from the Atlantic Ocean to the valleys of the Ohio and the Mississippi. There were nearly 800,000 people living in Virginia, of whom 300,000 were slaves. It was the most populous state. Virginia had four-fifths of the population of all of New England and was larger in land area than all of New England. There are compelling reasons, other than size and population, why Virginia's role in the ratification process was pivotal to the adoption and implementation of the new charter. First, it was Virginia which had called meetings in 1785 in Alexandria and in 1786 in Annapolis to discuss the growing problems arising under the Articles of Confederation with regard to trade, navigation, and the common defense. The failures of the states to cooperate in any way in these areas underscored the weakness of the government under which the original states were operating.

Secondly, eight of the required nine states had ratified the new Constitution before the Virginia Convention. But the New York Convention would not begin for seventeen days after the one in Virginia, and the anti-Federalists there were led by Governor DeWitt Clinton. Virginia's action would have great influence in New York. Successful implementation of the new Constitution would be questionable indeed if the new federation was geographically separated. In other words, the new federation might include New England, then skip New York, include Pennsylvania, then skip Virginia and North Carolina, then include the states further south. Would that have been workable?

Lastly, for the first time the proposed Constitution was fully debated at the Virginia Convention. It was debated clause by clause and the debate provided the only thorough discussion of both sides of the controversy that took place. Nowhere else were opposing positions to the proposal argued by men of such power, learning, and dignity. Had the opponents prevailed, and they very nearly did, new flames of opposition would have broken out throughout the states.

Who participated in this great debate? Almost every living Virginia statesman since colonial times. It is easier to note who was not at the Convention. Washington was not there; he stayed in Mount Vernon. He was, of course, a probable choice for the first presidency. But although not there physically, Washington was the moving spirit behind the new Constitution. Madison, Hamilton, and Jay, authors of the *Federalist Papers*, were the drafters, the public advocates, and the fine tuners, but Washington was the leader. His influence was ever present during the Richmond debates. If Madison was the quarterback, Washington was the coach.

Richard Henry Lee had declined to go to Philadelphia and he also declined the offer to be a candidate for the Virginia Convention. It is said that the water in Richmond disagreed with him. His serious reservations about the proposed Constitution were made known through daily and active letter writing to those assembled in Richmond.

Thomas Jefferson was in France. Time and distance prevented the type of daily influence that Lee and Washington were able to exert through their correspondence. Jefferson had friends on both sides of the debate and his replies at different times to different people sound somewhat Delphic, midst philosophical detachment.

It appears, however, that during the formulation and adoption of the Constitution, Jefferson deplored the secrecy of the Philadelphia Convention and expressed more faith in the general public than was held by many of the new Constitution's principal proponents. Jefferson was fearful of the creation of a hereditary autocracy, and saw the Society of the Cincinnati, established by Washington's officers, who mostly supported the new Constitution, as the possible source of such an autocracy. But he believed that a stronger central government was needed for the making of treaties, the conduct of commerce, and for all matters concerning foreign nations. Also Jefferson believed that the document adopted at Philadelphia should be strengthened by a Bill of Rights.

In sum, Jefferson approved of the open debates of the Virginia Convention. He would not have been at all surprised by the brilliance of the Virginia debates; he knew the people on both sides well. At times he held views compatible with both the proponents and opponents of the new Constitution.

Who was to attend the Virginia Convention? The General Assembly of Virginia determined that the Convention would consist of 170 members: two delegates from each of the eighty-four counties in Virginia, and one member each from Williamsburg and Norfolk. One might generalize about those elected to serve. As the Convention began, there appeared to be nearly an equal division between advocates and opponents, or Federalists and anti-Federalists. On the Federalist side were merchants, plantation owners, and lawyers. They came mostly from the Tidewater, from the Northern Neck, and from the Shenandoah Valley. Opposed to the Constitution were small farmers, advocates of paper money, and debtors. They came from Southside Virginia—almost everyone south of the James was opposed—the Piedmont and the area beyond the Alleghenies that today comprises the states of Kentucky and West Virginia. The opposition was not cohesive. There were those led by Patrick Henry who viewed the new Constitution as a catastrophe and a threat to the individual states and the rights of the individual citizens. There were others such as George Mason who viewed the Philadelphia version as a first draft with weaknesses that could be cured by amendment. From the beginning, this divided view probably determined that proponents would prevail.

Among the opponents, there appears to have been little organized effort in the selection of candidates for election to the Convention. The same can be said for the selection of members who would be candidates to preside over the Convention, for the determination in advance of who would speak when and on what subject, and what the overall strategy of the opposition would be. On the other hand, the Federalists were superbly organized. Candidates were chosen with great care; speakers were selected with purpose and planning. There was an overall strategy that ultimately prevailed, if only by a few votes, despite the fact that a majority of Virginians were opposed to the Constitution, as were a majority of the members of the Virginia General Assembly.

There appears to have been an almost equal division among the most able of Virginians who were prepared to debate the ratification. Among the supporters were James Madison, Edmund Pendleton, George Wythe, George Nicholas, John Marshall, and Lighthorse Harry Lee. Among the opponents were Patrick Henry, George Mason, William Grayson, James Monroe, John Tyler, and Benjamin Harrison. Each group of opposing parliamentary leaders represented a combination of older statesmen and young officers of the American Revolution.

We should note that relatively few of the 170 members spoke. For the most part the debating was done by six or seven speakers from each side. Also, despite the brilliant oratory of Patrick Henry, who spoke nearly a quarter of the time, the highly organized arguments of the Federalists contributed to the fact that more opponents than proponents changed their minds. There were those who believe, and I agree, that more votes were changed outside of the Convention than by debate.

What was to be debated? The proponents led by Madison had a strategy that repetitively featured certain themes.

- First, a strong central government with a strong executive was necessary for survival of the new republic.

- Second, that the individual states were not disposed or equipped to agree upon trade and commerce among themselves or with foreign nations, or to provide for the common defense.

- Third, that a national judiciary was necessary to interpret national law.

- Fourth, that the future of the union was at stake, the alternative being chaos.

- Fifth, that a number of states had already ratified the plan and Virginia should join them.

What were the themes of the opposition? Patrick Henry believed that the Philadelphia Constitution would be detrimental to Virginia and would fail to protect the rights and liberties of the people, as well as result in the loss of the Mississippi through a treaty with Spain. George Mason was more specific. Just after the end of the Philadelphia Convention, he wrote out his objections to the new Constitution. Mason was a brilliant and prophetic man and many of his proposals were subsequently dealt with, if not during the ratification process.

- First, the tax power should be restricted. (Well, he didn't succeed there!)

- Second, the size of the House of Representatives was inadequate to provide truly representative government.

- Third, the senators would not be representatives of the people, yet they would have great power with treaties, appointments, and impeachment. Their longer terms and the Senate's status as a continuing body could destroy balance in government.

- Fourth, the federal judiciary, as proposed, would destroy the state judiciaries.

- Fifth, the president would have no constitutional counsel.

- Sixth, the office of the vice president was unnecessary and his presidency of the Senate dangerously blended the executive and legislative power.

- Seventh, the unrestrained power of the president to grant pardons might be exercised to screen from punishment those whom he has secretly instigated to commit crimes and thereby prevent a discovery of his own guilt. (That was written in 1787 and is not a contemporary partisan statement.)

- Eighth, the declaration that all treaties are the supreme law of the land would give the executive and the Senate an exclusive power of legislation.

- Ninth, the capacity of a majority of the states to make commercial and navigation laws could bring economic ruin to the southern states, because it restrains the states from taxing their own exports. Also, the importation of slaves could not be prohibited for twenty years.

- Tenth, there was no section preserving liberty of the press or trial by jury in civil cases.

- Eleventh, there was danger in having standing armies in times of peace.

The anti-Federalists were fearful of the powers given to the new executive. They feared the treaty power, the command of the Army, the method of electing the president, and the failure in the Constitution to limit the president's term of office. They feared despotism and foresaw an elective monarchy.

Now let us proceed to the debate. The Convention began in Richmond on 2 June 1788, at the old Capitol, a wooden structure not large enough to accommodate the delegates. Richmond at that time was no more than a dusty town, two hundred houses, three or four large buildings and only one decent inn. The Federalists moved with precision at the beginning of the Convention. Edmund Pendleton was elected chairman. The anti-Federalists dared not oppose him and suffer an early defeat. The only person who might have defeated Pendleton was George Wythe, but he had also declared for the Constitution, and was later selected chairman of the committee of the whole. So the Federalists were assured of friendly presiding officers who could recognize speakers at times consistent with the overall strategy of the proponents.

On June 3 the Convention was moved to the Academy, the largest and most spacious building in Richmond, but not large enough to accommodate the crowds that came to hear the debates. The resolution of Congress calling for the Philadelphia Convention was read, also the report of that Convention, the resolution of the Virginia Assembly of October 1787, and the Act of Assembly convening the Virginia Convention. The Federalists thus established the authority to ratify. The struggle began.

George Mason rose to be recognized by the chairman. He presented a handsome and imposing figure, six feet tall, dressed completely in black with beautiful white hair and dark eyes. When Mason rose, no proponent sought to be recognized because the Federalists wanted the anti-Federalists to fire the first shot. Mason moved that the Constitution be discussed freely, clause by clause. Madison, smiling to himself, happily concurred. Many believed that Mason's initial move sealed the fate of the debate, arguing that the best chance of defeating the proposal would have been to attack it as a whole. But we must consider Mason's motives and the difference in his position from that of Patrick Henry.

Mason had been in Philadelphia, and while he had written the objections that I've read to you, he was in no position to oppose all of the Constitution because from the beginning he had been committed to write the best Constitution possible. Therefore, he wanted the entire Constitution discussed for amendment purposes. Besides, Mason and Henry both wanted time. They wanted to stall the ratification as long as they could to allow Mason's logic and Henry's passion sufficient time to work upon the delegates. John Tyler moved that the Convention resolve itself into a committee of the whole. Mason concurred, and the motion carried.

The next day the Convention met as a committee of the whole and George Wythe was called to the chair. George Wythe was America's first law professor. He had taught many of the delegates to the Convention. He had taught Thomas Jefferson and John Marshall. But, before Wythe could direct the clerk to read the preamble of the Constitution, Patrick Henry rose and asked to be recognized. He moved that the Acts leading up to the Convention, particularly the Act authorizing the Federal Convention in Philadelphia, be again read. It was apparent that Henry had no intention to abide by the "clause-by-clause" terms of Mason's resolution. His purpose was to attack the proceedings at Philadelphia as illegal, observing that the Articles of Confederation had not been amended as directed. Instead the Framers had written a new document.

Henry's old adversary, Pendleton correctly anticipated those intentions. He rose to oppose the reading, arguing briefly but forcefully, that the only Act of Assembly to be debated was the Act convening the Ratification Convention. That Act, the latest word from the people's representatives, was paramount in prescribing the action of the Virginia Convention. Henry, sensing the mood in the hall after Pendleton's forceful argument, withdrew his motion. Wythe now had the clerk read the preamble and the first two sections dealing with legislative power and the House of Representatives. George Nicholas took the floor to explain those sections.

George Nicholas represented Albemarle County along with his brother Wilson Nicholas. He was not a pretty man, squat with fat bulging around his neck; his physical appearance was certainly no match for his brain power, though, because he was a forceful and brilliant lawyer. (Those of you who watch television might think of Ed Asner and you will have some idea of what I believe George Nicholas looked like.) For more than two hours he held the attention of the members, as he masterfully covered the sections assigned to him.

At last Patrick Henry, greatest orator of his time, took the floor to speak. He did not respond to Nicholas; instead he spoke as if his motion to place the validity of the Philadelphia Convention before the present delegates had passed. He attacked the Constitution for having been written contrary to the instructions of Congress, representing an alteration of the entire government, for beginning "We the people" instead of "We the States," and for being presented at a time when the public's mind had been at repose. Henry asked why the drafters had done what they had no power to do.

Instantly Edmund Randolph was on his feet. (Edmund Randolph was the governor of Virginia.) He and George Mason had refused to sign the new Constitution at Philadelphia, and it was generally supposed throughout Virginia that he opposed the Constitution. But correspondence between George Washington and Edmund Randolph, unknown to the citizens of Virginia, had changed Randolph's mind. And a letter from New York, suggesting that the opponents of the Constitution in New York and Virginia should work hand in glove together, was under lock and key in Randolph's desk to be transmitted not to the Convention, but to the General Assembly of Virginia when it convened twenty-two or twenty-three days later.

Randolph was handsome and aristocratic. He had been Virginia's attorney general, a member of Congress, a delegate to the Annapolis meeting, and to the Philadelphia meeting. He said, "Never had such an event occurred without war or force." Randolph reviewed the state of the country under the Articles of Confederation. Congress was powerless, the public credit was ruined, treaties were violated, trade was paralyzed, justice trampled underfoot. The world looked upon Americans as unable to retain their democracy. The Union was at stake and Randolph was for the Union. Randolph's first open declaration for the Constitution was a mortal blow to the anti-Federalists.

Mason sought to lessen its effect. He immediately attacked the power of the new federal government to tax directly and predicted that such a power could destroy the state governments. He then stated that he would support conciliation if the direct tax could be removed by amendment. This was not the type of fighting talk after Randolph's defection that the anti-Federalists needed. Madison took the floor to say again with a slight smile that he "would welcome any conciliatory plan." The debate ended for the day.

40

The first full day of debate had gone badly for those against the Constitution. Henry and Mason seemed at cross purposes. Governor Randolph had come out for the Constitution, while the Federalists had moved with precision and purpose. Madison and Pendleton appeared to be well in control, but the Federalists were apprehensive, and with reason, about the capacity of Henry to influence the men from Kentucky who might well determine the final result.

The next day the chamber was crowded. It was expected that Madison would resume the next morning. He did not. He sent word he was ill. Was this a tactic? Perhaps so. More thunder than James Madison had was needed to follow Patrick Henry. The proponents called upon the state's most eminent jurist, and then Virginia's most dashing soldier. Edmund Randolph spoke first, feeble in body but powerful in argument: "Who but we the people had better authority? The choices were between a strong union and a weak confederation," he concluded. At his age nothing but the public good influenced him.

Pendleton was followed by Lighthorse Harry Lee, a young dashing hero of the Revolution, and a perfect contrast to Pendleton. How wisely the Federalists chose their speakers and when they would speak! Harry Lee said he hoped that Patrick Henry had come to judge and not to alarm. The bad condition of the country was due to the weakness of the Articles of Confederation.

When Patrick Henry rose to reply, he gave what many observers say may have been his finest speech. He skillfully hammered these points: It was the despised confederation that had carried us through the Revolution; sovereignty of the states, trial by jury, freedom of the press, human rights, and privileges would be imperiled, if not lost, if the confederation were to be abolished; a standing army would execute the commands of tyranny; the Constitution squints toward monarchy because a great and mighty president would have the powers of a king; if ever the president violates the law, he will come at the head of an army to carry everything before him; states that had hurriedly ratified the new plan now were regretting their haste and having second thoughts.

Henry had talked for three hours. He had made a profound impact upon the members of the Convention.

Moreover, he had moved the debate to his terms. The entire next day was used by the proponents in an effort to meet Henry's arguments. First, Randolph spoke for two hours, calling himself a child of the Revolution. He stated that the only choice was between adoption or dissolution of the Union.

He was followed by James Madison who gave the first of a series of masterful addresses about the proposed Constitution. Madison was a little over five feet tall and he had a squeaky voice that could hardly be heard in the chamber. He would have never survived politically in an age of television. His notes were held in his hat, which he held out before him as he spoke. He had to stand on tiptoe so he could be seen by all in the hall. He said that the new government was experimental, partly federal and partly confederated in nature. The powers of the federal government were enumerated, thus limiting the government to only those functions. Also the proposed government differed from the confederation. The power of the confederation rested in the legislative bodies of the different states while the powers of the new government were derived from a higher authority, the people. Madison, in his quiet manner, and with great logic refuted much of Henry's passionate argument.

Nicholas, who Henry reputedly feared more than any other speaker, closed the day. He chided Henry's fear of northern influence and said that all direct taxes paid would only be proportionate. He added that because Henry thought the ten representatives allocated to Virginia were insufficient, he was arguing that Virginia, by opposing the Union, have none at all. The proponents had fired three of their biggest guns.

The following day Henry called upon Randolph to complete his remarks so that he might understand why Randolph had changed his mind and what he had to say now in defense of the new system. Randolph replied with a lengthy statement and was followed by Madison who gave a brilliant speech reciting the history of many ancient and more contemporary federations and confederations. Then Henry rose and held the floor for the remainder of the day. He taunted Randolph who had stated that it was too late in the day to reject the new plan. Henry thundered that it was never too late to save all that is precious. Randolph had perhaps inadvertently used the word "herd." Henry seized on it, twisted it, substituted it for "We the people," and said it was the people who would be transformed from respectable, independent citizens to abject, dependent, subjects or slaves. When Henry finished, the Convention rose.

For the first week of debate, Henry alone had stood up to the combined skills of Pendleton, Madison, Randolph, Lee, and Nicholas. Except for one speech by Mason, he had no help. The Federalists were organized, but Patrick Henry had no talent for organization. Yet for a week he had dominated the floor on his terms, and the agreed upon clause-by-clause debate had yet to begin.

On the following Monday the rival forces returned for the second week of debate. As if symbolically, Henry and Mason walked arm in arm from the Swan Inn to the Convention to show the solidarity of the opposition forces. Henry resumed the floor. He was prematurely old at fifty-two. He wore an ill-fitting wig that was askew half the time and, as his portraits show, his glasses were often perched above his forehead. He always began rather quietly, then slowly rose to a crescendo after the first hour. Speaking almost haltingly, he asked about the future of the Mississippi River.

The Mississippi was the western boundary of Kentucky. Kentucky was part of Virginia, and Kentucky had fourteen members at the Convention who might well decide the fate of the new plan. Henry had heard of secret meetings in Congress in which seven states had voted to relinquish the river to Spain. The six southern states had opposed this. He asked whether the cession by treaty to Spain, as described under the new Constitution, would be possible under the new system? Would Randolph enlighten us as to this? Then for three hours he turned to the arguments of the proponents. As to Virginia's security, there is nothing to be feared from France, Spain, Holland, or for that matter from Maryland or Pennsylvania, or from the Indians. "You will sip sorrow," he promised, if you want any security other than the laws of Virginia. The national expenses will be increased tenfold; you will have to support a standing

army, a powerful navy, and support a long and rapacious training of officers and other troops.
What will be left for the states to do? Take care of the poor? Repair and make highways and bridges? For what purpose should state legislatures be continued? And then Henry hit upon what was to become the issue of the entire Convention. He warned against relying upon subsequent amendments. Madison had predicted that Henry's ultimate strategy would be to insist upon amendments prior to ratification. Madison believed their adoption would endanger the Constitution and lead to disunion. Henry was now attacked by Lee and then Randolph. Lee suggested that Henry had not seen sufficient military service to delve in military questions. Randolph, stung by Henry's questions about his late support for the Constitution, reacted angrily. It was said that seconds called upon Henry and Randolph that evening, but a duel was ultimately averted.

The second week of debate continued with Henry still controlling the tempo and the argument. But new speakers appeared. James Monroe, thirty years old and a former soldier, spoke against the Constitution. John Marshall, another young veteran, spoke for the new plan. Benjamin Harrison, representing the old aristocracy spoke against it. Madison spoke at length about the need for direct taxation. He was followed by George Mason who replied to Madison, but argued now almost as generally as had Henry. Another new speaker presented a general speech attacking the new plan on all fronts. He was William Grayson, considered by many the most gifted of the Virginians, although his name has disappeared from the history books. He was Oxford educated, a soldier of distinction, and regarded along with Nicholas as the finest debater in Virginia. He was answered by Pendleton, then Madison.

Henry returned on the next day to the subject of the Mississippi. He called on the members of Congress (there were four members of Congress who were also members of this Convention) to discuss the secret sessions regarding the agreement with Spain. Madison and Lee argued that the rights to the river would never have been given away. Monroe and Grayson differed and confirmed Henry's earlier speculations about secret understandings. Henry then made a speech describing what he thought the Mississippi Valley would look like after the Spaniards were through with it. He described what would happen in the worst possible terms and conjured visions of that lush, beautiful land being laid to waste. Pendleton was so overcome he was unable to respond. Nicholas responded lamely. Members from Kentucky were outraged and inflamed. That night Madison wrote a gloomy report to Washington at Mount Vernon.

After two weeks of debate, Henry finally allowed the Constitution to be discussed clause by clause. Here Madison's real genius showed through as he unfalteringly described how the new plan would work. Finally the members came to the last great issue of the debate—the judiciary. Opponents were counting on converting votes because of the universal fear of national courts. Pendleton was ill but he led off for the proponents. Mason, not a lawyer, replied. Finally, the young John Marshall stood and in masterful fashion laid out how the national judiciary would work. Refuting charges, he calmly answered all of the questions raised by Henry, Mason, Grayson, and Monroe, and was backed up by Madison.

Here an exchange took place between Mason and Madison that I should relate to you; you can think about it for what it's worth. Mason, in the midst of his speech, said that this Constitution was only the first step in a process by which those who were for strong central government, through court decisions, would use the judiciary to slowly change the Constitution to suit their will. Madison was offended, immediately jumped on his feet and asked for some detail. Mason retreated and what might have been a powerful argument against the Federalists was lost in the midst of the debates.

The end approached because opponents knew they had failed to score points or convert members during the judiciary arguments. Henry prepared to offer forty amendments including a Bill of Rights. By that time the proponents of the Constitution recognized that they too would to have to offer amendments even if they did not favor voting on them before the Constitution was adopted. So Wythe presented approximately the same number of amendments, including a Bill of Rights.

The difference between the two groups' proposals was that Henry wanted to vote on his amendments prior to ratification and then submit them to the other states. Such action by Virginia's Convention would have thrown the ratification process into chaos. But Wythe, supported by promises from Madison that the amendments would be considered in the First Congress, didn't propose more than a resolution favoring the amendments.

Henry rose to make his final speech. He said what he thought would happen if these amendments were not adopted in advance of the Constitution being ratified. At the height of his passion a storm arose in Richmond. Lightning began flashing, thunder began rolling, and the people in the hall retreated for a time. It was great showmanship, if not arranged.

The Federalists chose a man for giving their final argument who had not previously spoken. His name was James Innes. He has vanished from history, but was recognized as a brilliant orator. Innes spoke concisely in favor of deferring prior action on the amendments. Wythe then moved that the Constitution be ratified. John Tyler rose and offered Henry's amendments to be voted upon prior to ratification. Now came the vote that decided the issue. The counties were to vote alphabetically; counties first and then the two boroughs.

After Northumberland County the vote was sixty to sixty. After Randolph County, now a part of West Virginia, the vote was sixty-nine to sixty-nine. When the vote reached eighty-two to eighty, Edmund Pendleton, who had counted many a vote in his day, knew that the Constitution was safe, with regard to the adoption of any prior amendment. Remaining to vote were Westmoreland County, with Lighthorse Harry Lee and Bushrod Washington; York County with John Blair and George Wythe; Williamsburg with James Innes, Norfolk with Thomas Matthew, all supporters of ratification. The final vote was eighty-eight to eighty against Henry's prior amendments. A switch of five votes would have changed the history of adoption of our Constitution.

Then came the vote for ratification. A member from Chesterfield County switched and the vote was eighty-nine to seventy-nine for ratification. On June 27 the Convention met for the last time. George Wythe reported for the amendments committee that a Bill of Rights and twenty other amendments be recommended by resolution to the Virginia members of the first Congress under the new Constitution.

One of the amendments was to alter direct taxation. There was a motion to strike that amendment but Pendleton and nine others voted with Mason and Henry against the motion to strike: a small sop to the losers at the bitter end.

David Mays, the distinguished biographer of Pendleton, said the people of Virginia had been brought into the new federal union against their will. What might have made it different? Of course, a change of five votes would have made it different. A number of circumstances might have changed history: if the opponents had been more active and careful when delegates to the Convention were being selected; if Mason and Henry had adopted a more coherent strategy; if Washington had not convinced Randolph to alter his views; if Governor Randolph's position had been known prior to the Convention; if young John Marshall had not been so brilliant and logical in defending the judiciary clause; if the votes from Kentucky had not been split (they went ten against the Constitution and four for it), or if Henry, as he had threatened to do, had walked out of the Convention before the ratification vote was taken, the history of adoption of our Constitution might have been different. After the votes, Pendleton offered gracious remarks about how happy he was to serve with a new generation of younger Virginians who in the debate had performed as brilliantly as the old people who would not be around much longer.

Was there an epilogue? Certainly. Henry was in control of the Virginia General Assembly. When the time came to elect Virginia's first two senators, William Grayson and Richard Henry Lee defeated James Madison. Both had opposed the Constitution. Madison, despite the fact that his congressional district was gerrymandered to assure his defeat, somehow defeated Monroe as the first congressman from their district. True to his word, Madison introduced the Bill of Rights. He added the ninth and tenth amendment to rights spelled out in Mason's Virginia Bill of Rights. They were immediately adopted. Henry, who had sought a new Convention to consider the Constitution, abandoned his efforts and went home to practice law and tend his crops.

We in Virginia have seldom lost an opportunity to take pride in anything. Certainly we may take pride in the caliber of the ratification debate on both sides. And if you weigh what Mason and Henry accomplished indirectly, much of it taken care of in future years, you may certainly take pride in the caliber of political genius of those who argued on both sides in Richmond nearly two hundred years ago. Thank you.

QUESTION: How were the state legislatures persuaded to surrender whatever authority they might have had to a special Constitutional Convention, and secondly, how much overlap in Virginia was there between members of the General Assembly and members of the Convention?

SENATOR SPONG: I can answer your first question very quickly: I don't know. I don't understand how the anti-Federalists allowed that to happen. Secondly, there was a great overlap. By great, I mean as many as twenty-five. One of the questions that hung over the Convention and was later taken up in the Assembly concerned a time overlap. If there was an overlap, with the General Assembly coming to town as the Convention ended, would the members who served in both bodies receive double pay? That occupied quite a bit of discussion as soon as the General Assembly convened.

QUESTION: Do you have any explanation for Madison's opposition to a Bill of Rights until forced to do otherwise?

SENATOR SPONG: I came here hoping somebody would ask that. Madison believed that it would be a mistake to spell out the rights because there might be rights that came to us under Magna Carta, under the British common law, and under our heritage as a nation that might be said not to exist if they were not explicitly spelled out in the Constitution. There is correspondence between Madison and Jefferson in France substantiating that. But Madison learned a political lesson in the senatorial elections. He knew that, aside from honoring what he had promised at the

Convention, the majority of people in Virginia wanted a Bill of Rights. He was not opposed to a Bill of Rights as such; he was worried about its effect.

Now what he did is interesting. He added a Ninth Amendment which said the listing of specific rights did not preclude the existence of other rights that might have come to us through the common law tradition. Those of you who listened to the Bork confirmation hearings will know the Ninth Amendment is important because of the right to privacy, or the public's right to know—which along with First Amendment rights is used in many cases involving media in the courtroom—may be derived from the Ninth Amendment. That is what Madison intended. And in the Tenth Amendment he added a reserve clause about all things not enumerated and spelled out in the Constitution being reserved to the states.

Madison was not against a Bill of Rights; he simply did not think it wise to specify all of those rights.

COMMENT: The importance of Virginia was probably far greater than it has been given credit for in some other parts of the Union. Alexander Hamilton was fearful that New York would not ratify because Governor Clinton was an anti-Federalist. But the following year New York went on to ratify by about twenty-three votes.

SENATOR SPONG: It would have been defeated in New York, I think.

QUESTION: Without Virginia?

SENATOR SPONG: I'm not certain, but I believe the letter, locked in Edmund Randolph's desk and transmitted not to the Convention but to the General Assembly when it convened almost after the fact, was significant in changing New York's vote. It also affected Randolph's political career. Initially, Randolph was appointed the first attorney general of the United States. Virginians had two of the original Cabinet of four: Jefferson and Randolph. Randolph's star seemed to shine in the firmament but declined. Many believed that not transmitting the New York request to work together with the Virginia anti-Federalist forces was improper.

QUESTION: Bill, I'm always intrigued by the age of these people. My understanding is that most of them were under forty, except for one person. What was the age group?

SENATOR SPONG: You had several prominent members in their thirties but also many older ones. Randolph was still in his thirties. Innes was in his thirties. Monroe, Lee and Marshall were in their thirties. They were of the generation that had participated as soldiers of the Revolution. And then you had the old-timers who were still alive—Wythe, Pendleton, Harrison.

QUESTION: They were in their fifties, weren't they?

SENATOR SPONG: Some of them were older. Mason was in his fifties; Henry was in his fifties. This is interesting from a medical standpoint; other than age, their size was astonishing. Except for Madison, they were quite tall when compared to the standard height of people at that time.

NARRATOR: Thank you very much, Senator Spong, for your presentation.

SENATOR SPONG: Thank you.

Thomas Jefferson and the Language of Liberty

ALF J. MAPP, JR.

NARRATOR: Last November Alf Mapp wrote in a note, "I tried to present a fresh interpretation of Jefferson and at the same time examine his philosophical legacy to the Republic." Those two elements, fresh interpretation and the philosophy of Jefferson's practice, are characteristic of his Book-of-the-Month volume, *Thomas Jefferson: A Strange Case of Mistaken Identity.* The book has received impressive acclaim, selling out at nearly every book store at which it has been displayed; almost all of its twenty-three reviews have been totally complimentary. There was one review—and there had to be one—in that group which asked a few sinister questions, but the jury is now in on the book that Alf Mapp described last November, and the response has been enormously favorable.

As many of you know, Professor Mapp is an eminent scholar and professor at Old Dominion University, and I think it is high time that the University of Virginia drew on the resources statewide in fields of concern to the University and to the Miller Center. Several of his books have gone through a series of editions and continue in print: *Frock Coats and Epaulets; The Golden Dragon: Alfred the Great and His Times; The Virginia Experiment: The Old Dominion's Role in the Making of America, 1607-1781;* he is co-author of *Chesapeake Bay in the American Revolution* and, in another genre, *America Creates Its Own Literature.* He has taught both literature and history in both departments of Old Dominion.

I had the sense, when we met in 1981, when he was named a Virginia Laureate, that he was the closest to being a Renaissance man that I had seen for a long time. He is a *summa cum laude* graduate of William and Mary; he was editorial writer, associate editor, and editorial chief for the *Portsmouth Star*; he has been news editor and editorial writer for the *Virginian Pilot*; he was a member of the editorial board of the Jamestown Foundation and of the Commission for the 350th Anniversary of Representative Government in the Western Hemisphere. He was chairman of the Portsmouth Revolutionary Bicentennial Commission, member of the Scholars Advisory Committee for the War of Independence Commission of Virginia, and consultant for the federal Bicentennial Reenactment of the Battle of Yorktown. He was national president of the Order of Cape Henry. He hosted a TV series, *Jamestown to Yorktown*, in the 1970s. He twice received the Outstanding American Educator award.

In every sense Alf Mapp is one of Virginia's proudest sons, both in the field of journalism, in which his career began, and in the field of creative writing, in which he has continued. He was nominated, for instance, both for the artist's and for the scholar's award of Phi Kappa Phi. His sponsors finally decided to concentrate on the scholar nomination. His kind of versatility is rare in American higher education, and we feel privileged, therefore, that he has stopped at the Miller Center and will talk to us for a little bit this morning about Jefferson and Jefferson's conceptions of liberty.

PROFESSOR MAPP: Thank you very much. If I were half as intelligent as Ken claims I am, I would not open my mouth at this moment; I would claim to have gotten laryngitis and would rest on that introduction. But I guess a little sneaky streak of honesty forces me to go ahead and reveal my limitations.

I must say that I am rather hesitant to speak on Thomas Jefferson and the language of liberty here at the University of Virginia, the very citadel of Jeffersonian scholarship, formerly graced by Dr. Dumas Malone, whose presence still lingers here. His meaningful presence in the world of scholarship will linger for foreseeable generations, along with the work carried forward by Professor Peterson,

Professor Mayo and others. We must not forget the fact that Ken Thompson, through this very institute, has helped to make the thinking people of America and of some other nations, aware not only of the problems faced by Jefferson in his presidency, but also of the problems faced by virtually every person who has occupied the position of chief magistrate in this country. If you begin to discuss any president, you run into various resources that have been made available to us through Ken's activity. Of course, I appreciate doubly compliments coming from a person of his stature.

Thomas Jefferson was an artist. It is often said that he was an artist as a sideline. He has been spoken of sometimes as an artist who wrote. Yet when we discuss Thomas Jefferson in the language of liberty, we are talking not only about his literary gifts but also about something very central to his philosophy, or we might even say his philosophies since they varied according to the different periods of his life. Jefferson was, moreover, a very conscious artist with words. I say "conscious artist" with some justification: there is a letter that Thomas Jefferson wrote to Tom Paine which he concluded by saying that he believed his correspondent to be the best writer then living in America "with the possible exception of your obedient servant, Thomas Jefferson." I think history has largely conceded the truth of that comment.

Students of American literature today say that Thomas Jefferson, Benjamin Franklin, and Thomas Paine—if we may call him an American—were the leading American writers in their time. Scholars observe that Jefferson and Franklin were both substantive in their writing. As a matter of fact, a distinguished European writer on the Enlightenment has said that as important as Voltaire and certain other figures were to that movement, if you want an understanding of it at its best, you can not do better than turn to two Americans: Thomas Jefferson and Benjamin Franklin. So they were both distinguished for substance.

Thomas Paine, of course, was a lively writer, a great sloganeer. He could have made a fortune in the advertising business in our day and might have chosen to, but he was not quite as long on substance or depth; he was not really a man of scholarship. One thing that may surprise us, perhaps, is that Paine said he seldom read a book in his mature years. He just was too restless to read full-length books, but he enjoyed good, clever phrases.

However, Jefferson at his best matched Paine in liveliness and had, at the same time, the substance of Benjamin Franklin. So literary critics today say that Thomas Jefferson was the best writer of his day. He was, as you know, also a good candidate for best statesman of his day and the best architect of his day. Of course, the most notable examples of his architecture are available to you here, and you are very fortunate in that respect. Besides being, as you also know, the American pioneer of paleontology and an important linguist, Jefferson did many other things which often have been enumerated.

No doubt you have heard quoted many times John F. Kennedy's statement when he entertained American winners of the Nobel prize: "I think this is the most extraordinary collection of talent, of human knowledge, that has ever been gathered together at the White House—with the possible exception of when Thomas Jefferson dined alone." Well, all that is quite true, and being a first-rate writer was one of the most important of his talents.

A major thesis of my book *Thomas Jefferson: A Strange Case of Mistaken Identity* is that Jefferson was by aptitude and temperament an artist, but because of the values of the society of which he was a privileged member, he disciplined himself to become a statesman. He had great powers of self discipline in everything except spending for luxuries; that was one thing in which he couldn't discipline himself. Yet he did have tremendous powers of self-discipline, and he also had a mind of such various capabilities that he easily became one of the foremost statesmen in the world in his time.

This is an interesting subject for speculation. You know scholars who have studied the life of Abraham Lincoln say that they believe it is probable that, had Lincoln lived in another place and another time, he would have chosen a literary career. He loved putting words together more than he did anything else, and even though he was able to devote very little of his time to this in his most active years, he still was far better at it than most people who had chosen it as a profession. They point out that, as

Lincoln was growing up on the frontier, he became an extremely ambitious man. We are very fortunate that Lincoln was a great humanitarian, because otherwise he would have been very dangerous with his great ambition. He was determined to excel. There were two routes to success on the frontier: the law and politics, and often they were combined; therefore Abraham Lincoln pursued those fields.

I think it equally probable that we would be safe in taking Jefferson at his word when he said that if he had to live his life over, he would wish that it were possible to devote his days to science. During the celebration of the bicentennial of the American Revolution, there was a special exhibit on Jefferson and science provided by the federal government in Washington, and over the entry to that exhibit was that quotation from Jefferson about wishing to devote his days to science. What they didn't take into consideration is the fact that in Jefferson's day the word "science" meant learning, any kind of scholarship. If you were studying the plays of Shakespeare, that would be science; if you were studying the sculpture of Rodin, that would be science. All of these things would have been called "science." So what Jefferson was really saying was, "If I could do it over, and it were possible, I would like to devote my days to writing and scholarship."

Thomas Jefferson, being a brilliant writer and a very subtle one, and one familiar with every literary genre, took full advantage of the rich connotations of English that make it such a great vehicle for poetry and for all kinds of imaginative literature. The French maintain that their language is a better one for writing laws and scientific treatises. They secretly, of course, think it is better for everything, probably, but the French say it is better, particularly for those purposes, because it is impossible for an educated person to misunderstand the meaning. There are not the little extra nuances and reverberations; there are not as many varied connotations as with the English language. And of course we know that those who love Italian and Spanish, which is certainly easy to do, say that they are far more beautiful languages than English. Still there are many linguists and writers who say that English is much richer in varied resonances than other languages. All

55

the little associations that can be in one English word can give it great poetic meanings. Thomas Jefferson was fully aware of this and he used language for poetic effect many times. He did in his letters and in some of his speeches.

At the same time, if Thomas Jefferson was preparing a public document, he would use language with great precision in philosophical definition. Thomas Jefferson, in any case, was an extremely exact man. He kept precise records on everything. It was George Washington whose last conscious act on his deathbed was to take his own pulse, but we could easily picture Thomas Jefferson doing the same thing. Jefferson, grief-stricken at the death of a loved one, found himself calculating how long it took the gravediggers to dig the grave and how long it would take them to dig the entire plot. If it had been his own grave, he would have done the same thing. He was an exact man, indeed.

Only on his honeymoon, and then only for a single day, did Thomas Jefferson become so absorbed in his daily life that he failed to make notes in his account book. Even at Blenheim, which was the last rest stop that Jefferson and Martha made on their journey through the snow to their first night at Monticello, Jefferson noted that the remaining distance—the distance between Blenheim and Monticello—was eight and one one-hundredths miles. He thought it necessary to record that because most of the people in the neighborhood thought it was really eight miles.

Here, then, was a man who indeed used words with conscious specificity. We have all too often assumed that certain terms that Jefferson used in the Declaration of Independence were there simply because they had an appealing sound, because they fitted in with the rhythm, and that he used them for that reason. And it is true that he was quite aware of the sounds of language; it's true that he used the rhythms gracefully. Yet he was using the terms in a very specific sense. For instance, when he wrote, "We hold these truths to be self-evident," many people assumed that he was simply saying, "This is something anybody knows." Behind all this, though, was the entire tradition of the Enlightenment to which Thomas Jefferson had been introduced—I suppose it is not heresy to say this—to which he had been introduced at the College of William and Mary. Later on Thomas Jefferson wanted to be sure that other people were introduced to this tradition at a great state institution, and therefore, of course, we are fortunate to have the University of Virginia.

Thomas Jefferson was quite familiar with the works of Francis Hutcheson. Hutcheson loomed much larger in the consciousness of intellectuals in his own day than now. We tend frequently to forget about the Scottish influence in the Enlightenment except for a little nod at Hume now and then (and then partly because there are a number of amusing anecdotes about him that can enliven our topic). But Hutcheson was recognized as a master thinker of the Enlightenment and he wrote a great deal about self-evidence. He maintained that there were a number of things that clearly would not be self-evident; they had to be the products of learning. If people could divest their minds of prejudices, though, there was a certain inborn recognition of right and wrong. Even children start very early to distinguish between what is fair and what is not fair. As subjective as the standard is, it is sometimes the one who is imposing on the other who really recognizes that there is some sort of standard of fairness. There was a belief that this standard was inborn; some said it was a platonic ideal. Jefferson himself did not use "platonic ideal" because he had an intense dislike of Plato. (By the way, none of us have ever been able to find out why Jefferson had such an intense dislike of Plato; occasionally he uses ideas that obviously derived from Plato, but he did not like the man. He liked Aristotle much better.) Jefferson used this term "self-evident" in the very strict Enlightenment sense.

When Jefferson wrote, "All men are created equal"—and incidentally it is clear from the context of Jefferson's use of the word "men" on many occasions that he was referring to both sexes—he also had a specific meaning in mind. While we might think Jefferson backward in his reference to the sexes by modern standards, he was, in this as in most things, far in advance of most people in his time. He took great care, for instance, to ensure his daughters' education. Even the great statesman Talleyrand in Paris, which was then considered the center of the intellectual world, said: "It is surprising that Mr. Jefferson takes such care for the education of his daughters; they are girls!" In this way, Jefferson was far in advance of most in his time.

Now it has been noted how very strange it was that Mr. Jefferson said on one occasion that it was a pity that women might ever have anything to do with politics, which seems to be something that we would resent right away. It is just as strange to see in another place that he says it's a pity the scholars ever have anything to do with politics. Of course he certainly considered himself a scholar, so his comment about women may not have been any indication that he believed they were unfit for a political role, but rather that politics was an unfortunate business for either women or scholars to spend their time on. When David Rittenhouse, the scientist from Philadelphia, was pressured by political responsibilities, he wrote, "I am satisfied there is an order of geniuses above that occupation and therefore exempted from it. . . . I doubt not there are in your country many persons equal to the task of conducting governments, but you should consider that the world has but one Rittenhouse." This attitude partly expressed Jefferson's attitude toward politics as well. Yet Thomas Jefferson, as we know, revered many figures who had brought wisdom to the process of government, and he did admire the ideal of the philosopher-king, despite the fact that he didn't want to refer to Plato. For our part, I think we have to agree that Thomas Jefferson comes nearer to the ideal of the philosopher-king than anyone else who has ever been president of the United States.

Regarding this exact use of language, we should give credit to Gary Wills for pointing out many of the similarities between what Francis Hutcheson said and what Jefferson was later to argue. Mr. Wills says that he thinks it very unlikely that Thomas Jefferson had ever read John Locke's *Two Treatises on Government.* Therefore, he thinks most of us who have been writing about Jefferson for years are somewhat misguided. (He said this before my book came out, but he would still say the same thing; there is nothing in my book that would change his view.) He thinks we have assumed the influence of John Locke on Jefferson, and he believes part of the apparent influence is mere coincidence. Wills says it is unlikely that Jefferson read Locke's *Two Treatises on Government* because these were not very widely circulated in America. It is true that Locke's treatises were not very widely circulated in America at the time, but they were circulated. I think it is extremely unlikely that Thomas Jefferson, with his consummate intellectual curiosity and his great concern for government, should have failed to read the twin treatises in political philosophy that comprised one of the two most important works produced by one of his three chief heroes.

When Jefferson was secretary of state, he kept three portraits in his office, those of Bacon, Newton and Locke. On one occasion when Alexander Hamilton was in Jefferson's office, Hamilton looked up and said, "Who are they?" Jefferson replied, "They are the three greatest figures in the history of the world: Bacon, Newton and Locke." Alexander Hamilton looked very serious and then pronounced his opinion: "Julius Caesar was the greatest man who ever lived." Based on this story, it is quite obvious that these three men were Jefferson's chief heroes. If Locke was one of his three chief heroes in world history, and if there was a copy of Locke's treatises available in America, it is inconceivable that Jefferson would not have been familiar with them. We can document his pertinacity in obtaining any number of things. When he wanted to get a certain kind of sheep dog to bring back to America, Jefferson, who had trouble moving over rugged terrain, climbed up what was at times an almost perpendicular wall of a mountain in Europe to bring back specimens. He was a very determined man once he was started on something.

In reference to the traveling, though, it is ironic that Thomas Jefferson, who did more to open the West than anyone else, not only by the great Louisiana Purchase but also by the Lewis and Clark expedition, and who was more aware of the West and its significance than any other great American statesman, never traveled more than fifty miles west of Charlottesville. He was unlike his father who had gone on wilderness expeditions and on one occasion had slept in a hollow tree. But to Mr. Jefferson's credit, he did have difficulties with balance which made travel by water almost impossible; it was at great personal sacrifice, therefore, that he finally accepted an appointment as United States Minister to France. Traveling over the rugged terrain west of Charlottesville was similarly hard on him.

Before we forget about Hutcheson's influence on Jefferson, though, I want to cite one brief passage of which

I think you will find echoes in the Declaration of Independence. Francis Hutcheson wrote:

> As the end of all civil power is acknowledged by all to be the safety and happiness of the whole body, any power not naturally conducive to this end is unjust, which the people, who rashly granted it under an error, may justly abolish again when they find it necessary for their safety to do so.

One can point out any number of passages in Jefferson's writing that sound very much like John Locke, any number that sound very much like Francis Hutcheson, and various other thinkers. There are some comments that are like those of James Wilson, and some like those of George Mason. Shortly after the Declaration of Independence appeared, some people made this charge. John Adams, who had had more to do with Jefferson being the writer of the Declaration than any other person, said, "That charge misses the idea completely." I'm paraphrasing this, but Adams said, "Mr. Jefferson did not sign the Declaration of Independence as its author; he signed it simply as one representative of his state subscribing to it, the same as everybody else who signed it. Thus, it would have been a mistake if he had tried to be too original because he was to express the sentiment of the entire group. He was to put into this document everything of any significance that had been said and subscribed to by other participants in the Convention, who also had been influenced by these philosophers. Would you have had him bring less learning to the task?"

It is interesting to note, however, how Adams's perception of authorship changed at a later date when he and Jefferson were on opposite sides politically. A newspaper, on the occasion of Independence Day, praised Thomas Jefferson as the author of the magnificent phrases in the Declaration of Independence. John Adams wrote in effect, "It's not original at all; all the phrases have been taken from other members of the Convention and from famous philosophers." Fortunately though, as you know, John Adams and Thomas Jefferson later repaired their differences. In the mellowness of old age, when someone again noted that there was nothing very original about Jefferson's Declaration of Independence, Adams said, "Of course not, it wasn't supposed to be. It's exactly what it was supposed to be; it represents the best thinking and the best words for the time."

Thomas Jefferson did grow up as a figure of the Enlightenment and he remains a significant figure of the Enlightenment. Yet sometimes we are inclined to think of him not just as a representative of the Enlightenment, but as typical of it. I think that's a mistake because Thomas Jefferson was too independent and versatile a genius to be typical of any particular group. There has been an effort in subsequent years, as in his own time, to "pigeonhole" Jefferson.

Some politicians, particularly those who wish to serve a conservative cause, have pointed out what Mr. Jefferson said about concentrations of federal power, and depicted Jefferson as being a thoroughgoing conservative. On the other hand, in journalistic and in academic circles there has been a tendency to picture Jefferson as an undeviating liberal. Actually Jefferson in his approach to public problems came very near to doing the same sort of thing that Associate Justice Lewis Powell recently said he had tried to do as a justice of the Supreme Court: to address each question on its merits and not worry about what ideology prescribed on a given issue.

There were, however, consistencies in Jefferson's beliefs. For instance, he was always for individual freedom; you can follow that all the way through his thought. But there are times when his opinion would seem to be conservative, and other times when it would seem to be liberal. Of course, I realize we are on dangerous ground if we try to say what is "conservative" and what is "liberal" because some of us have lived through a time when those who called for intervention in Korea were labeled liberals because they were concerned with the United States' international responsibilities. Then, just a few years later, those who wanted the United States troops to remain in Korea were "conservatives," because they didn't realize that you should not be intervening in movements toward freedom in other lands. Thus a position that had been "conservative" in the one case became "liberal" in the other and vice versa, so we are always being subjective when we use these labels.

Thomas Jefferson did alter some of his Enlightenment beliefs. For instance, a cardinal principle of the Enlightenment was the belief in the ultimate perfectability of man. Jefferson moved from a cautious endorsement of the ultimate perfectability of man to the conclusion that the chief function of government was to protect man from himself. Here one can see that there was an evolution in Jefferson's thought.

Let me illustrate this diversity of thought. It's interesting sometimes to take quotations from some of the Founding Fathers and try to guess who said them. We can frequently do this with great accuracy. Let me give some background to this quotation. In August 1776 there was a proposal for direct election of United States senators. That proposal lost, as you remember, and the senators were elected by the state legislatures. From the style and the sentiment of this quotation, which Founding Father would this be?

> I have ever observed that a choice by the people themselves is not generally distinguished for its wisdom. This first secretion from them is usually crude and heterogeneous. I could submit, though not so willingly, to an appointment for life, or to anything rather than a mere creation by and dependence on the people.

Until I found out the truth, I would have guessed these were the words of Alexander Hamilton. They are actually Thomas Jefferson's, so we see Thomas Jefferson did not always have a complete reliance on the wisdom of the people. Yet I think this is reasonably consistent because he said on one occasion that if we hoped to have a democracy in which people could remain free and ignorant at the same time, we would be hoping for what had never been and never would be. Of course, Jefferson wanted to spread the blessings of education; he wanted more and more people to become qualified to vote. Sometimes we hear speakers say that the greatest danger to our democracy now is that potential voters are ignorant and apathetic. Mr. Jefferson would have admitted that this was a very great danger, but he would have urged us to be thankful that the ones who are ignorant are also apathetic! Mr. Jefferson would have wanted them to try to educate themselves before they cast their ballots.

I once had a very self-satisfied friend who didn't pay much attention to public affairs, or rather, took a quite lordly, disdainful attitude toward them. He would say, "Well, I've just done my civic duty. I have voted for three candidates. I didn't know anything about any of them, but I've done my civic duty." I think there are many people who still feel that way, but Jefferson would not have been pleased.

Jefferson, however, was not a cynic; he was relieved from being a cynic partly by his temperament. He said that he always liked to take things by the "smooth handle" whenever that was possible. He found that most things had both a "rough handle" and a "smooth handle." Jefferson was one who liked people and wanted to believe the best of them.

Jefferson also had historical perspective. A sense of history can be very valuable to a statesman. It can exist in a scholar of history, or it can sometimes exist in one who is not a scholar, but who has thought deeply about history, such as Abraham Lincoln. Someone such as Winston Churchill fits into both categories. Robert E. Lee, in his last written message, said, "History teaches us to hope." Well, it doesn't with all people, but history did teach Thomas Jefferson to hope.

I think this sense of history is an important thing that we are in danger of losing now. One member of the faculty of the University of Virginia has written a book [*Cultural Literacy*] that I'm glad to see is very popular now. It points out some of the deficiencies in education from the beginning on up. One of the great dangers we face is that so much of modern education, both in the preparatory schools and universities, destroys the idea of continuity and hence the idea of cause and effect. We see more and more courses that are planned simply to be thematic. I think there is a place for thematic courses, but some people say with pride, "We have deliberately eliminated the chronological approach." The result, as a recent survey indicated, is that nearly one-third of high school students in the United States, when asked to choose a time frame for the discovery of America by Columbus, chose a date after 1750. I think that tells us a great deal. I don't think—although I try to remember them myself—there is any great virtue in the average student remembering a tremendous number of specific dates. However, he should know which historical figures are contemporaries. Students should not think that perhaps Benedict Arnold knew Stonewall Jackson.

We find Jefferson bringing to the Declaration of Independence a universal sense in the very language of it. Most such declarations, when one group of people breaks off from another, are simply catalogs of complaints. Of course there is that long section in the Declaration of Independence which documents our complaints against King and Parliament. Yet Jefferson's Declaration of Independence was lifted far above that level by its very opening words: "When, in the course of human events." We immediately see that this document is not written just for a specific time and place; Jefferson was speaking to all times and all places. "When, in the course of human events": the marvelous sweep of those opening lines carries with it a sense of the sublime. History is important to us, of course, in teaching us about certain mistakes that we hope to avoid. History is important in giving us a sense of hope and also in giving us a sense of danger. But history has another function as well; history contributes a sense of the sublime in the same fashion as the very broadest and deepest studies of science. Astronomy, for instance, can give us a sense of the sublime.

Longinus, back in the old classical days, wrote about the sublime as something that gives us a sense of spaciousness in time or place, a sense of elevation above the ordinary. Matthew Arnold, likewise, wrote about it and popularized the idea again in the nineteenth century. Time and time again, when humanity itself has been called upon to make extraordinary sacrifices, and to rise to levels of nobility of which it did not believe itself capable, we have been influenced by words of sublimity. The words of the

Declaration of Independence carried that same sublimity that we often see in times of great peril.

When Abraham Lincoln in 1862 addressed the people of the United States in a moment of great peril, when he was calling upon them to assume heavy burdens and upon their elected representatives to make decisions that might threaten their political careers, he brought forth from them actions that many had predicted would not be possible. When he told them, "We cannot escape history. . . . the fiery trial through which we pass will light us down, in honor or dishonor, to the latest generation," that was sublimity. They were reminded of capabilities that they didn't realize they had.

Franklin Delano Roosevelt, when he wanted the United States to take the risk involved in lend-lease, had many logical arguments for it, but he also made an appeal to the sublime. The United States was not yet committed to joining Britain in the war, and many Americans still cherished the idea that it would be possible to come through those times in safety without doing it. While President Roosevelt gave some logical arguments, he didn't say, "I want you to tell your congressman that you expect him to vote for H.R. 1776, which provides for the exchange of overage American destroyers for the use of certain British bases." Mr. Roosevelt gave the logical arguments, but first he took his audience up on a high plain, swept by the winds of history, and he said, "This generation of Americans has a rendezvous with destiny," and chills went up and down their spines. Consequently, the American people responded in a way that many wise politicians had said they would not.

Then there was Sir Winston Churchill. I have a habit of quoting him perhaps even more than I should, but when I was a correspondent in my early twenties, I had the privilege of covering him on several occasions and he still is the most spontaneously eloquent person whom I have ever heard. You will remember that the experts employed by Churchill's own government had reported to him and to the Cabinet that there was every indication on the basis of a dispassionate study that if Britain continued to struggle against the Nazis, it would be crushed. Yet Churchill did not deceive his people. (Those days have been written about very beautifully by Ken Thompson in one of his books.) Churchill, with a kind of nobility we like to think of as old-fashioned but which has probably never been common in any age, did not deceive his people; he confronted them with the truth. He wanted to instill in them a feeling that they were a noble part of human history, that they must carry on the fight regardless of the consequences. Churchill told them, "Let us so bear ourselves, that if the British Empire and Commonwealth of Nations should last for a thousand years, men will still say this was their finest hour," and they made it their finest hour.

The gift of sublimity through language that Thomas Jefferson brought to public affairs is something of which our generation is once again sadly in need. We have a number of clever phrase-makers, but not many who can make chills run up and down the spine, who can make us feel that we are capable of doing more than logic tells us we can.

Jefferson was also a great man of logic. He could employ logic to prove anything in which he was deeply interested, but he was also a man of intense passion; passion in the form of anger against injustice, passion of love for his country, and yes, perhaps, for his lover, Maria Cosway, as well. He *was* a man passionate in all ways. He was a man who reacted with strong emotion, and though he believed that emotions should be submitted to wisdom, he also thought that emotions sometimes gave us intuitions which reason might well consider. Jefferson was not an ideologue; I think it would be very difficult to classify him as either a liberal or a conservative. This is true of most great minds.

Some people point to the Louisiana Purchase as a great inconsistency in Thomas Jefferson, something that his prior life would not lead us to believe to be consonant with his principles. He had the opportunity to double the size of the United States. Purchasing the Louisiana Territory was a marvelous bargain which he took advantage of, even though the Constitution did not specifically give him this power. Some have said that here he abandoned his convictions on strict construction of the Constitution because something was too good to pass up, that he resorted to Alexander

66

Hamilton's policy of broad construction. It *is* ironic that Alexander Hamilton, who talked repeatedly about broad construction, was Thomas Jefferson's foremost opponent; yet the man who first made broad construction a dramatic part of the Constitution by this single act was Jefferson.

Nevertheless, we can question whether this action was inconsistent. If we think that nothing in Thomas Jefferson's life led up to this, then we are mistaken. I have a few examples that I chose from my book. Back in August of 1787, before we have any evidence of Alexander Hamilton having written specifically about broad construction, Thomas Jefferson seemed to support it himself. At that time some said that Congress lacked the power to enforce the levies on the states to support the government. Jefferson argued for that power. He was an opponent of too strictly interpreting the Constitution, but he wasn't a fanatic about it like Alexander Hamilton. In 1790 when Hamilton brought forth his "assumption scheme" and said that we could find no clause in the Constitution authorizing Congress to assume the debts of states, Mr. Jefferson noted that there was nothing prohibiting it either.

Going back to the time when Jefferson was representing this nation abroad, there was a crisis with the Barbary Pirates when it looked as if word from America would not come instructing him and Adams on how to react in defense of American rights. Adams assumed that nothing could be done. Jefferson argued that, in the absence of word from Congress, they should assume that they had the right to do what was necessary for the security of the United States. So one cannot simply contend that Jefferson was always against a broad construction of the Constitution. He was not an ideologue; he was quite liberal in believing in educating as many people as possible; he was quite liberal in believing that there should be no economic and social barriers to the acquisition of an education by anyone who had the natural ability for it; he was certainly liberal in his belief in individual freedom. Yet by our present standards, in his belief that the federal government should not do things that the state government could do and the state government should not do things that the local government could satisfactorily do, and that the local government should not do anything that the individual could do for himself, he might be called conservative. It is impossible to pigeonhole him. In fact we find Jefferson going back and forth between what could be called a liberal position in one instance and a conservative one in another. In some instances he cites certain traditions that he considers powerful and nourishing that should not be relinquished. In other instances he is looking forward with a strong exploratory sense and he is forecasting and initiating growth.

This is one of the most important aspects of government; it is one thing we should always take into consideration. I'm talking about it so much that I think some of my friends may be calling it "Mapp's law." I think that the vitality of any civilization, the vitality of any culture or subculture, is dependent on maintaining a very delicate balance between the pull of tradition and the urge to exploration. Of course, there isn't time to fully explore the details of this now, but I think if you will consider Egyptian civilization in the fourth dynasty and the greater part of the eighteenth dynasty, Babylonia under Hammurabi, Athens in the fifth century, B.C. (that glorious century), the Italian cities of the Renaissance, England in the Elizabethan and Jacobean eras, and the United States in the Revolutionary and early federal periods, you will find that there was always a great awareness of tradition. They feared the idea of cutting away all the roots. For instance, the great American Revolutionary leaders were constantly harking back to the influence of Greece and Rome. Here was Thomas Jefferson who, even while planning for the future and leading the nation into unprecedented new areas, chose the Palladian as an architectural model, with its important influences of the old Greek and Roman. This, I think, shows how his philosophy was a blend of both classical conservative and romantic progressive.

Pascal said that all human misery came from people being unable to sit quietly in a room. Well, that's one way of looking at it. Some people *are* always trying to rip up things and do away with tradition. On the other hand, though, if people remained always quietly in rooms, it might be a sort of slow death. I think of this in connection with Toynbee—Ken has an excellent book on Toynbee—who once gave an example of this from the experience of Britain's

North Sea fishermen. The herring that they brought in were fine, first-rate fish in every respect. Gradually, though, the places where the herring congregated got farther and farther from the British shores, so that the fishermen had to remain longer at sea with the catch before they could bring them in. Eventually they filled large tanks with sea water to keep the herring alive and they said, "We will bring them back and it will be just as if they were still in the sea." But it wasn't just as if they were still in the sea. They were not the healthy, vigorous herring that they had been when they were first caught. On one occasion, though, the fishermen opened one tank and found that the herring were in first-class condition. They discovered that by mistake somebody had left one of the herring's natural predators in the tank—not enough of the natural predators to overwhelm the herring, but one to make them a little insecure, to challenge them. I'm told that, to this day, when fishermen bring back the herring catch, they put a natural predator in the same tank.

Few of us today would vote to have a natural predator thrown into our midst. Yet some impartial arbiter of our destiny probably should throw a natural predator among us now and then, not an overwhelming one, but a challenging one. We thrive on challenge, and that makes us work on maintaining that important balance between drawing nourishment from tradition, and, at the same time, reaching for something new.

I'm not going to go into detail now, but this phenomenon is observable in every phase of life that we know about. The scientists tell us that amoebae, those humblest of creatures, seem to thrive best when, with one of their little, irregular, and constantly changing protrusions, they appear to reach out to where they have come from and with another portion of their bodies reach out to where they are going. One can make an analogy to civilizations: the ones that thrive the most seem to be those that are not letting go of the past because so much of that is essential, but at the same time are reaching out to grasp something new.

To return to Jefferson, there is much talk now about constitutional change and about going back to the intent of the Founders. Thomas Jefferson, as you well know but most of the American public does not, was not at the Constitutional Convention, at least not physically. Yet he had conferred a great deal, in person and in letters with his friend, James Madison, who is known as the Father of the Constitution. He had influenced so many others by his thoughts—and this influence can easily be traced—that in a sense he was present there.

One of the beautiful things in examining the relationship between Madison and Jefferson was to see how they affected each other philosophically. Madison from the very beginning did not believe in the perfectability of man. He didn't believe that was attainable. He had grown up in a Calvinist family, and he was aware that there was a certain amount of wickedness in human beings. Thomas Jefferson had grown up in an Anglican society which at that time in Virginia chose to ignore these things. Madison kept warning Jefferson that one has to protect people against themselves. Man wouldn't be good when just left alone; he wasn't always bad because someone had been tampering with him. Madison had his impact, but fortunately Jefferson made Madison much more hopeful too, so it worked both ways.

This is what Jefferson, near the end of his life, wrote on this matter of constitutional change. As he foresaw so many things, he anticipated the argument that we must be *governed*, not just *influenced*, by the intent of the Founders. Jefferson would agree that we should only be *influenced* by their intent. These are Jefferson's words:

> I am certainly not an advocate for frequent and untried changes in laws and constitutions, but I know also that laws and institutions must go hand in hand with the progress of the human mind. As that becomes more developed, more enlightened, as new discoveries are made, new truths disclosed, and manners and opinions changed with the change of circumstances, institutions must advance also and keep pace with the times. We might as well require a man still to wear the coat which fitted him when a boy as civilized society to remain ever under the regimen of their barbarous ancestors.

70

In one respect Mr. Jefferson was just a bit too optimistic. Remember he had lived into that century of optimism, the nineteenth century. He was already expressing, in advance of Tennyson, a belief in progress akin to the Victorian laureate's idea of each generation as "heir to all the ages, foremost in the files of time," and the concept that the course of humanity would be constantly onward and upward. It hasn't worked out quite that way, and of course to that extent Jefferson was too optimistic. Yet I think he was a little nearer the truth than many indulging in the pessimism which is so common today. Some say we are having crisis after crisis and that we will ultimately be destroyed by it, but this is too pessimistic.

I still think about the herring that Toynbee wrote about. I have another example. I have a Chinese neighbor who has shared with me some of the teachings of his people and some things about the characters in which the Chinese language is written. He has shown me the character for the word "crisis." Do you know how the Chinese characters are compounded of other characters with their own individual meanings? The Chinese character for "crisis" is compounded of the one for "danger" and the one for "opportunity." We are destined, so long as our civilization survives, to encounter dangers repeatedly. There will be crisis after crisis, but the crisis that brings danger can also bring opportunity. I think that Thomas Jefferson, if he could give us an aphorism that would be consistent with most of his philosophy, would say that we should never ignore the danger, but we should never fail to perceive the opportunity.

NARRATOR: I think we'd all agree this is quite a way to begin our year at the Miller Center. We didn't quite know how to classify Alf Mapp's lecture. The Miller Center is interested in rhetoric and discourse, and his talk fits there. In this bicentennial year, we are increasingly interested in constitutionalism, and Professor Mapp certainly explores topics in that area. We are also interested in the impact of Europe on America and America on Europe in the broader area of political thought. Professor Mapp has touched on all of these issues and more in his insightful talk. I'm sure many of you who were stimulated with the discussion may want to avail yourselves of this opportunity for a few questions.

QUESTION: Did Mr. Jefferson at any time foresee or demonstrate any concern about the great proliferation of cultures, customs, and languages that we are experiencing now in America as a threat to our unity?

PROFESSOR MAPP: He thought that there might be such a proliferation. He appears to have thought that there would be a little more time for assimilation than has turned out to be true in modern days. He didn't foresee certain conditions of transportation in the world and so forth that would make this difference. There were people who were alarmed in Jefferson's time because he was encouraging people from France, Germany and Italy to settle in the United States and indeed in Virginia. Many were quite worried that this would be overdone, and that the whole character of the area would be changed. After all, Mazzei had been brought over from Italy and was wearing Italian hunting jackets, and then people all over Albemarle County began wearing the same cut of jacket. Some people wondered how far this would go. As another example, when the progenitor of the DuPont family in the United States came from France to this country, several federalist newspapers said that this was a great danger because the DuPonts would stay here in the United States, become citizens, and they would be a radical influence in this nation!

In truth, Jefferson did not foresee the situation you talk about. Jefferson, I think, would have been concerned about some aspects of our current problem. He believed that the United States should become a haven for intellects from all over the world. Of course the United States served that function to a great extent in World War II, and this has happened under other conditions as well. Yet Jefferson did not want the basic Anglo-Saxon culture to change too quickly. He was perhaps the most inter-nationally-minded of our presidents, certainly among the three or four most internationally-minded. At the same time, whenever he said "my country," he meant Virginia.

In his later years, he said that no young man should be sent over to the universities abroad, particularly those in Paris. (He said this partly because the sight of Parisian women would be too distracting, which says a little about his own inclinations.) His fear was that they would move, perhaps, too far away from the ways of their own people. Immersion in other cultures should come later in their education, not when they were very young. I think Mr. Jefferson would have been pleased that great intellects and artists would be attracted to America from different parts of the world. If he found that the Anglo-Saxon culture was changing too rapidly, he would have thought it too great a loss of stability; he did say some things of that sort. Of course if he had grown up in our time, he might have had other concerns.

I'm trying to tell you as honestly as I can what I think he would have thought. That is one problem I have had as Jefferson's biographer; some people are quite disturbed if you document Mr. Jefferson's views on something that you don't consider to be an ideal thing to say now. I have tried to report what he actually said and not only those things I would now consider ideal by contemporary standards.

QUESTION: I would like to ask you why you think it was that there was so little apparent rapport between Virginia's two greatest representatives in the Revolution—Washington and Jefferson? I never particularly thought of it, but I wondered whether perhaps you took the view that Washington was by nature a Platonist and Jefferson was by nature an Aristotelian?

PROFESSOR MAPP: That's interesting, and I am not surprised that the classicist Arthur Stocker has made such a distinction. I hadn't thought of that myself.

I do know that at first Jefferson had an almost reverential love for Washington. Jefferson had lost his father who was a great hero to him when he was a boy, and he was always looking for a father figure as a young man. He seemed to find that figure in George Washington.

Incidentally, there is increasing evidence that Alexander Hamilton and Jefferson were both looking for father figures, and that each of them found one in George Washington. This may have contributed to the rivalry between the two of them. Each thought that Washington was being unfair to him in the interest of the other one; that was one source of their antipathy. Jefferson, as secretary of state to Washington, found himself increasingly in disagreement with the rest of Washington's Cabinet, and Hamilton seemed to dominate that Cabinet. Jefferson said that the Cabinet was divided in sentiment three and a half to one and a half between what was later known as the Federalist philosophy and the Republican philosophy. He said that in the case of Edmund Randolph, who served in the Cabinet first as attorney general, that he would see things first one way and then the other way, so you ought to count him one-half on each side. (I think this is one of the instances that shows we are quite wrong when we assume that Jefferson had no sense of humor. Incidentally, he carried a humorous book with him whenever he went on long travels and showed a sense of humor in many other things.)

Over and over Washington expressed his fear that the Revolution might continue beyond what it had been, that there might never be the stability the nation needed. Hamilton fed this fear, and there is also very great evidence that Hamilton fed Washington's fears about Thomas Jefferson. Many people have assumed for a long time that Jefferson was very unfair to Hamilton when he said that Hamilton really wanted a return to monarchy. But Gouveneur Morris, who delivered the oration at Alexander Hamilton's funeral (a close friend of Hamilton's), had confided to his diary the day before something which confirms Jefferson's claims. He wrote of Hamilton, "He was in principle opposed to republican and attached to monarchial government." So Jefferson was probably right in that.

Hamilton was a brilliant man and a man willing to sacrifice himself in many ways for patriotism, but at the same time he did not give Jefferson any leeway; he was quite unfair in many things. Once Jefferson unwisely wrote some criticism of Washington that he did not want to become public. It was written confidentially to a friend, but it finally reached the ears of Alexander Hamilton.

Hamilton saw to it that Washington learned about this, thus widening the breach between them. One of the great sorrows of Jefferson's life was that when Washington died, he still believed that Jefferson had become his enemy.

Years later when Jefferson was asked to write about Washington he said that he was one of the few truly great men in history. Jefferson was not as cynical as the compiler of a biographical dictionary of the early 1800s which I own. His sketch of George Washington opens with the statement, "Unlike most great men, George Washington was not a criminal." Jefferson was not that cynical.

QUESTION: This is scarcely a fair question, but what do you think Jefferson's reaction would be today to the confirmation of Judge Bork to the Supreme Court?

PROFESSOR MAPP: This would be an impossible thing for me to say. I just wouldn't have any way of knowing. I know that Jefferson theoretically believed that all shades of opinion should be represented on the Supreme Court. He always believed this until any matter about which he was deeply concerned was being considered by the Court.

I will give you just one brief example of how Jefferson, in a very human way, could change his attitude about things. At one point in 1787, the newspapers were being very supportive of Thomas Jefferson. Jefferson wrote—you've often heard this because newspapers like to remind us of it at least once a year—"The basis of our government being the opinion of the people, the very first object should be to keep that right. Were it left to me to decide whether we should have a government without newspapers, or newspapers without government, I should not hesitate a moment to prefer the latter."

In 1799 some of the newspapers were giving him a bit of a hard time, and Jefferson modified his view a little. Writing to Elbridge Gerry, he said, "I am for . . . freedom of the press and against all violations of the Constitution to silence by force and not by reason the complaints or criticisms, just or unjust." He is admitting that the press is sometimes unjust, but insists that we still shouldn't silence it. Later in 1799 he writes, "To the press alone, checkered as it is with abuses, the world is indebted for all the triumphs which have been gained by reason and humanity over error and oppression."

Then in 1804, when the press had been giving him a rougher time, he said, "The firmness with which the people have withstood the late abuses of the press, the discernment they have manifested between truth and falsehood show that they may safely be trusted to hear everything, true and false, and to form a correct judgment between them." By 1807 they were giving him a very hard time indeed, all over the country. Then he wrote, "It is a melancholy truth, that a suppression of the press could not more completely deprive the nation of its benefits than is done by its abandoned prostitution to falsehood. . . . Nothing can now be believed which is seen in a newspaper." Finally in 1820 he said, "I read but one newspaper and that . . . more for its advertisements than its news."

In 1823 the newspapers saluted him as a grand old man, and he wrote to Lafayette, "The only security of all is in a free press. The force of public opinion cannot be resisted when permitted freely to be expressed. The agitation it produces must be submitted to. It is necessary to keep the waters pure." This only shows that Jefferson, a brilliant man of very strong character and much more fair-minded than most, was still human and at times subjective. I can't possibly say what he would have said at this time about Bork!

QUESTION: There is a somewhat narrower topic which also deserves mention, specifically the evolution of Jefferson's ideas on slavery. What do you know of his views on the subject?

PROFESSOR MAPP: Thomas Jefferson, as some of you may recall, wrote into his draft of the Declaration of Independence a pledge on the part of the nation to abolish slavery. The document itself, the Declaration of Independence, did not abolish slavery but there was this pledge. Jefferson argued that it was contradictory for us to say that we were basing our demand for independence on the fact that we had God-given rights as human beings and also to say that we had a right to enslave other human beings. What isn't well known is that this pledge was deleted not only because of the attitude of some of the southern planters (who said that their economy would collapse if they didn't have slave labor), but also because some of the gentlemen from New England said (though they were opposed to slavery) that this Declaration of Independence would be meaningless unless it had the support of the most influential people in all of our states. Unfortunately a majority of the most influential people in their states had made their money in the slave trade, and they were not going to accept a declaration that pledged us to the abolition of slavery. Their idea was to neglect the issue then and to fight one battle at a time. Jefferson did not give up on the idea of returning to the slavery issue later.

Of course Jefferson took great delight when, in 1776, the Virginia Convention made Virginia the first state to abolish the importation of slaves; Virginia went that far. There was also a move to go ahead and eliminate slavery within the state, but it failed. Jefferson advocated that proposal, and at one time that measure came to within a few votes of passage. Think how different history could have been if it had been passed. Jefferson's idea was that emancipation should be a gradual process with reimbursement of the slave owners, which is exactly what Abraham Lincoln called for at a later date. In both cases people said the proposal was too costly. Of course we see what a great error that was.

Jefferson was consistently opposed to slavery, but the thing that troubles some people is why he continued to own slaves himself. The answer may lie in the fact that there was a law in Virginia at that time that all free slaves had to leave the state. Realistically, Jefferson wondered where they would go. They would either go to other states where people could take advantage of them or they would go out into the western lands where they were ill-equipped to deal with the situation. He thought that as long as he was alive, they were probably better off as his slaves.

Slavery is a very bad thing under any conditions, but Jefferson's version of slavery was a little different from the usual practice. His slaves had days off—there were some other planters that did this—on which they could earn income of their own. I found one interesting little item on this topic in Jefferson's account book. Once when he went to the theater to buy his tickets, he found that he had no money with him. So he turned to his slave who had driven him into town and borrowed the money from him. The next day he paid his slave back. This is a rather unusual situation when the master is borrowing money from a slave and then paying him back. Jefferson was apparently more consistent in his views about slavery than in nearly anything else, or at least consistent as in few other things.

NARRATOR: I'm sure I speak for everyone in thanking Professor Mapp. Given his great talents in lecturing, Professor Mapp—and his wife, Ramona, who has taught at Old Dominion University and is now an administrator at Tidewater Community College—are sure to be in great demand at their home university. Nonetheless, I hope this is only the beginning and that there will be many more visits by the Mapps to the University of Virginia. Perhaps along the way they also can help to weld and unite the University of Virginia more closely with other institutions like Old Dominion. Thank you very much.

The Presidency and the
Constitutional System

CONGRESSMAN RICHARD BOLLING

NARRATOR: Some years ago Congressman Bolling wrote in Volume V of *Papers of Presidential Transitions and Foreign Policy*:

> As I look back and think ahead to seek ways of improving the effectiveness of governmental systems, divided, complex, and always in transition, I am convinced that it is a mistake to examine any one political phenomenon as if it took place by itself. There must always be an attempt to at least set the stage, to look at the past and to examine the short and long range consequences of a particular political event. Politics is not a series of separate events; it is much more like a seamless web.

Congressman Bolling served as congressman from the Fifth District of Missouri during the tenure of eight presidents, from the Eighty-first to the Ninety-sixth Congress. He occupied a number of crucial positions as chairman of the Select Committee on Committees of the House of Representatives; chairman of the Rules Committee; chairman of the Joint Economic Committee; a member of the Steering and Policy Committee of the Democratic Caucus and of the House Budget Committee.

Lest you think that his background is exclusively that of the politician, academically he was Chub Fellow at Yale University and Fellow at the Center for Advanced Studies at

Wesleyan University and taught and lectured in Kansas City. He was a Lieutenant Colonel in the United States Army and received the Distinguished Congressional Service Award from the American Political Science Association. He probably is the only person who will read his text who was ever elected to the *Sports Illustrated* Twenty-fifth Anniversary All-American Football Team. He is the author of *House Out of Order* and *Power in the House*, which appeared in 1968 but is now in a revised edition.

CONGRESSMAN BOLLING: I'd like to talk a little bit about the last five presidents. I don't want to offend anybody, most particularly at the beginning, but I think that four of the last five presidents have been failures. They've been failures in utterly different ways. The one I do not consider a failure professionally is Jerry Ford, and that may be my prejudice because he and I were friends and still are, despite the fact that we disagree on virtually every domestic item one can think of. But we disagree in a way that is less than disagreeable. We disagree because we believe differently and we understand the political process. I had the opportunity to be very close to a few of the last five presidents, not very close to all of them, but I had the opportunity to observe all of them.

I didn't retire until after President Reagan's first two years with the Congress, but he wasn't the reason I retired. Circumstances kept me from feeling that I had to stay. I retired relatively young for a congressman, but with no difficulties or political opposition. I retired because I thought it was time to do something else. Basically, it was to try and help all of the people in academia who have devoted their lives to studying how government works.

I thought that my responsibility as a congressman was to lead and to educate, and I thought educate was the right word all the time. I still feel that way, but I found it much more difficult to do what I planned to do when I retired. The simple reason was that I still could learn. So I read a lot, particularly about the Constitution and constitutional history, and found it very difficult to come to a final conclusion. Fairly recently, I attempted a book and wrote a chunk of it and decided I didn't like it. I'm now on my fourth redraft, and you are going to get the benefit or the trouble of hearing my conclusions.

I supported a candidate who is now out of the Democratic race for the presidency. I supported him to avoid what I believe were the reasons why four of our last five presidents failed. I shall tell you what I have as positive recommendations for any president in the future.

Lyndon Johnson failed because he wasn't balanced. He tried to do too much. I happen to agree with what he tried to do in almost all the domestic cases. I think we were way behind on the things that needed to be done with the poor and the weak in society, but I think he overreached himself, and I think nothing could be done to stop him.

His successor, to my utter amazement, may turn up in history as professionally a pretty good president. He was a crook and I always thought he was a crook; I despised Richard Nixon. To say that he might turn out to be a pretty good president in retrospect is almost a shock to me. Nixon did great damage to the republic. The fact that a president could be forced to retire hurt the political process severely.

Carter came to Congress with many pleasant and some very good ideas. He was very bright and very able, but wholly incompetent to be president because he couldn't deal with Congress at all, ever. From the beginning he failed with Congress and alienated his congressional allies, virtually from his first days in office. I think he would have been a good president, by the way, in the second term because he learned a lot, but he was a terrible president in the first term. Aside from Congress, he turned off the American people and that didn't help.

Now I'm going to say very little about Ronald Reagan, but I'll say something rather definitive, and I'm going to say it right now: I think he is the worst president that ever served the United States of America.

There is one characteristic of all four presidents that I consider failed, and it goes against the myths of our time. Lyndon Johnson was unable to creatively work with the Congress. The great myth is that Lyndon Johnson was a genius with the Congress; the fact is that he never was even a successful legislator. He was a successful politician in the House; when he was in the Senate and became Senate

81

leader he was a great manipulator of senators. He did not deal very well with any constituency except his own Texas constituency. He did that rather well, though in ways that I did not always admire. But that is beside the point.

When he became president, he failed to pay attention to anybody when he created his programs, unless they were going in the direction that he wanted to go. And everything he wanted to do, he wanted to do in the first year of his elected presidency. He succeeded Jack Kennedy in 1963 and served through 1964 and the election, but only after he was elected president did he become overwhelmed by himself.

By that time, his friends who had had the power to check him in the past were either dead or gone. Sam Rayburn died in 1961 and he was the only person who could really sit Lyndon Johnson down. His great friend in the Senate, Richard Russell of Georgia, was no longer there to influence him effectively, and he listened to no one. His imbalance made him a failure, not just in Vietnam but also in domestic policy and, in particular, in economic policies. He couldn't and didn't work with the House, he just ran over it, and he tried to run over the Senate. He didn't learn from the institution.

Obviously, the same thing is true of Nixon. Nixon did a better job of working with the House, but he didn't work honestly with it. If you remember those days and if you watched events carefully, it was rather fascinating to see what happened. At first, the Committee on the Judiciary that dealt with the Watergate investigation was composed mostly of liberal Democrats who were concerned about Richard Nixon and what he had done. Then most of the moderate Democrats joined up, followed by the conservative Democrats. Eventually the most liberal Republicans were also swayed until virtually all Republicans were there as well. Even then some were still saying, that although they didn't really like him, they believed him. Still, there was a shift. The only time he really worked with Congress was the time when it was really working against him. He was never completely honest with the Congress; he never took advantage of all the people that could have helped him in Congress.

Carter was hopeless. I'm going to talk about this from the positive side. Carter had a legislative liaison team that honestly believed that the Congress of the United States was a little bit lower than the legislature of the State of Georgia. I grew up in north Alabama so I'm not anti-Georgia or anti-South. The liaison team simply didn't have any comprehension of what the House of Representatives was like; they did not even understand the constitutional sense of what the House of Representatives was supposed to be. They treated everybody as if they were slaves—people were supposed to automatically do what the President wanted. It was a disaster.

Mr. Reagan, on the other hand, was enormously successful with the Congress in the first year. You won't believe it because you don't get it in the press, but after that first year, he hardly ever won another fight. A few times he won on issues related to the Iran-Contra affair, but on economic issues, like taxes in 1982, the Republicans in the Senate turned against him. We passed a tax bill that did exactly the opposite of what Ronald Reagan wanted until he accepted it. He swore for months that he would never sign a tax bill that increased taxes, yet taxes were substantially increased in 1982, primarily due to the efforts of Senator Robert Dole. That is certainly interesting considering the way things are today.

For reasons of politeness, I'm not going into the rest of Reagan's eight years. I'm not sure that what I have to say would be completely balanced. I may not give him enough credit for cheering up the country. He did that. I may not give him enough credit for some of the things that have happened in foreign policy. Usually, it seems to me, good things happened despite him, but they have happened and they are very important.

So we have had, in my view, a disastrous breakdown in our system of separated powers starting after the death of Jack Kennedy. And in a system like ours, unless all the players understand that they must share power, we do not get a government capable of governing the country. The only time a similar breakdown occurred was during the Civil War, and obviously there was no government that suited all the people of the country at that time. That's the only time the political process has completely broken down.

The political process of this country is, in my judgment, the most difficult political process in the world. At least one can reasonably and honestly say, that we have popular government, free government, and democratic government with republican procedures.

We have a country so complicated that even when there were only thirteen states, you wonder how it came to be. You wonder how those people were able to put together the Constitution, and more importantly, how the document was ratified. The wonderful thing about the Constitution is that is was ratified. There have been many constitutions written in many places. Our Constitution was ratified and we have managed to remain at peace with ourselves and to develop and grow. This was largely the result of the capacity of the Congress, the president, and the Supreme Court to have some relationship with each other on almost every major occasion. I am saying, in effect, that you cannot have an effective government, no matter how bright a president is or how well-informed he is about the issues, unless he understands how to work with the Congress.

You may think that is fine as long as the Congress and the president are of the same party. We read a great deal about how our government has broken down because different parties control different bodies. Yet the greatest accomplishments of this country's federal government have been achieved with bipartisan support. Our victory in World War II was such an accomplishment. I guess there are a good many people who know that that war wasn't a cinch, that an Allied victory was not certain. There were, after all, two wars being fought, one in the Pacific and the other in Europe, and in each case there was a very good possibility that we were going to lose. Winning both wars was a bipartisan accomplishment, done with Presidents Roosevelt and Truman working closely with the Congress.

It is remarkable that when Truman faced a Republican House, most of the important things the Truman administration wanted to do in foreign policy and defense were done. The Eightieth Congress, which he used as a political whipping boy on domestic policy in 1948, was the Congress through which much of the great program went. On foreign affairs there was a residue of cooperative attitudes and an understanding that you had to work together. I am reasonably sure that at least in modern times, unless presidents are really able to work closely with members of the opposite party, they can't implement programs which will last. I think Johnson pushed his programs so strongly that there was a backlash which undid many of those needed programs. This could have been avoided if he had been more moderate.

The key is that presidents must understand how to work with the Congress, and in particular the House. Why is the House so important? The House is so important because it is the only federal institution in which all of the concerns of the American people have a reasonable chance to penetrate. The House doesn't just represent the great issues; the House represents the issues of people in congressional districts and the small lobbyists. The people who don't have lots of money or lots of numbers have an opportunity to talk to members of the House. That makes the House more difficult to deal with than the Senate, especially because there are 435 members rather than 100. Its complexity, though, is one of the reasons the House is so fascinating. When you pass major legislation in the House, you are consciously putting all the great interest groups of the country together, first in a contest and then in a cooperative effort. If presidents don't understand that, and don't work with the House on that kind of a basis, they cannot possibly work successfully with the government as a whole.

I could talk about the Supreme Court or the bureaucracy, and I am prepared to talk about a variety of other things if you ask me questions. There is one key point I want to make, and though it may sound just like an old, retired member of the House thinking about how important his work was, that really isn't the point. I believe firmly that this country has forgotten the role of the House. By and large, it is true not just for presidents but for the whole country. The academic community has forgotten it because most academics don't like to spend the time that's necessary to understand the House of Representatives and how it works.

I'll tell you an anecdote and then I'll stop. Years and years ago, the most distinguished of all the journalists of his time, Walter Lippmann, invited me to lunch. He invited me to a club that I wouldn't belong to for reasons that you may have detected in what I've said and what I will say. It amused me. It was a nice club and it was perfectly proper for him to be there, but it was not something that I was going to be involved in for several reasons. We had a lovely, wonderful luncheon which lasted four hours. I couldn't believe it. The last hour or so I was trying to get away because I just didn't believe that I should be taking up a great man's time. I didn't agree with Walter Lippmann on an awful lot of things, but I admired him. My press friends thought that he was a second coming of sorts. I don't mean to be disrespectful in saying that, but they really revered him. I didn't really know why he had asked me to lunch, but we spent a long time talking about nothing but the House. He asked the questions and I answered quickly and briefly.

For a long time I didn't hear anything and did what I did in the House. Finally I heard, as I knew I'd hear in time, why he wasn't picking up on anything we had spoken about and why I didn't hear from him again. Lippmann is supposed to have said, "You know, the young man was really very interesting. He said all kinds of things that I knew to be accurate and was giving me a really wonderful description of the institution. But I've decided it was just too complicated for me to get involved in and I wasn't going to do anything more about it."

I will submit to you that that's what all the media people have decided, with the exception of a few, and too many others have decided the same. Further, I would submit to you that if that isn't understood by either the people or the presidents, our system is going to break down. It isn't going to work unless we have presidents who understand that they have to work with the House and how to work with the House.

Jack Kennedy died having had the greatest congressional relations team there ever was. The Republicans in the Eisenhower administration and in this administration have had consistently good congressional relations. We shall need better congressional relations with the president if we are going to make the policy decisions we must make.

QUESTION: I recently read a book that claimed that Richard Nixon was brilliant in dealing with foreign policy and cited his recognition of China and agreements with Russia as examples. Would you agree with that assessment?

CONGRESSMAN BOLLING: Yes. I know less about the details of the Brezhnev agreements, but I do think that the opening with China was crucial and long overdue. I thought it was ridiculous that this issue frightened a lot of politicians. It didn't have to, but it did. However, the people weren't very frightened by the idea. A demagogue like McCarthy or Nixon, in his own day, could rouse up and frighten some people. But just plain ordinary, moderate people, given a chance, weren't shocked if you said you were in favor of opening relations with China. I always put it on a simple *quid pro quo* basis: We would certainly recognize China if they'd give us something in return. It didn't have to be anything tangible, simply an assurance, for example, that they would be friendlier, or let's say, less unfriendly.

QUESTION: Congressman Bolling, you have indicated how important it is for an incoming president to be able to work with the Congress. Is there anything on the other side, something that Congress needs to do? What do you see, particularly in the transition between election and taking office, that might be accomplished?

CONGRESSMAN BOLLING: I think Congress needs to do a number of things to improve the transition. I think there should be more money made available for a newly elected president, whether it is George Bush or some Democrat. There should be the opportunity to do some things very quickly, and it takes money to do that. The Congress already has a burden, in my opinion, to improve the formal transition—the approach to the transition.

The Congress has to have a sense of responsibility to the president. I don't think I exaggerate this; I think that the president almost calls the tune on how partisan Congress is by how partisan he is. I'm talking about Congress as an entity, as an institution. If the president is friendly and sticks to his word, and tries to be cooperative with both individuals and institutions, he'll ultimately get a pretty good reaction. If he is confrontational and determined to make political hay out of situations, it can get pretty ugly. But the president has the power to cool down that situation.

It got pretty ugly in the 1940s, in Truman's time. But Truman never lost the people with whom he had to work effectively in foreign policy and defense to get results. He would blast the Republicans on domestic policy and talk about the no-good Eightieth Congress, yet he maintained his relationships with Vandenberg and people in the House who were equally important. In order to get things through the House, he had to have the support of some Republicans.

I think the president has the initiative because he is, after all, the most powerful politician there is, and the most powerful legislator. Everybody forgets that the president is a legislator. I don't see how anybody can. He is a legislator because he has a veto, and all he has to do is veto something and he raises the ante almost out of sight. Getting two-thirds of the votes in the House, or in the Senate, is very different than getting the majority. That veto is a tremendous source of influence.

I'm not trying to put all the burden on the president. I would be shocked if a Democratic speaker did not respond to a legitimate, nonpartisan request from the president.

I don't know how it looks from the outside. The media deal with things as they wish, and I don't mean to be a media-basher. I worked with them very closely for many years. But the media just do not give Congress much of a chance to be understood simply because they don't have enough people covering it. There are probably only a half dozen papers in the United States that have real coverage of the House. The media cover what is relatively easy to cover. You can cover the president very easily. Sam Donaldson could cover the president by himself, and he will be able to supply the whole network with news about the president reasonably well. It isn't hard to keep up with the Supreme Court either; that also can be dealt with by one person. Similarly, one person can deal remarkably well with one hundred senators. The Senate is run entirely differently. But when you get to the House, you are dealing with complexity. I don't know how to solve that problem, but I think that's *the* problem.

I cannot conceive of a House Speaker in this era who would be an affront to the president. It happened to other presidents, Lincoln, for example, who was accosted by the radical element of his own party. Roosevelt too, had an incident or two when his leadership in the Senate resigned on him because he bad-mouthed a senator for what he had said about the wartime tax bill. Roosevelt was dead right, by the way; it was a lousy tax bill, but he shouldn't have made it known the way he did. In any event, that's all they could get and they had worked very hard on it. Alben Barkley resigned in a huff and Roosevelt had to beg him to come back. I recognize the problem. If Robert Michel [House Minority leader] turned out to be the Speaker and a Democrat were elected, he'd be just as worried about being good to the president as I would, or anybody else who was on the Democratic side.

COMMENT: To carry on the same line of thought, the House seemed to be easier to understand in the days of a very strong Speaker and a half dozen strong committee chairmen with whom the president might have rapport and considerable contact. The reorganization of the House seems to present, at least to the public view, the presence of a considerable array of power centers. Therefore, the institution is harder to understand and deal with. Looking at it from the inside, how is the House mobilized into effective majorities?

CONGRESSMAN BOLLING: That's hard to answer because you have to recognize a number of myths first. Some of you may know that I worked very closely with Sam Rayburn for the last ten years of his life. Sam Rayburn had very little power compared to the institutional power of Carl Albert, Tip O'Neill, or the current Speaker. Most of the time he was defeated by the committees. Sam Rayburn could only do what was possible, given the committee system. For the most part, the committee system of Congress was controlled by a coalition of conservative southern Democrats and almost all Republicans from 1938 until 1961. The Democrats from the South were conservative, the Republicans from the Middle West were conservative, and of course conservatives came from other places too.

The truth of the matter is that Roosevelt completely lost control of Congress from about 1939 on. Sam Rayburn was sort of his emissary who tried to do something with Congress. Rayburn had great power to change a few votes. He had gathered up his chips in the classic way. His power lasted the longest, I think, in the history of the House. He had been a committee chairman in 1931 and then Speaker until he died in 1961. I don't know of any other political career that was like that. I happen to believe that Rayburn was the greatest legislator of all time. But he didn't have all that power usually attributed to him.

The *institutional* power of the present Speaker is substantially greater. Rayburn looked powerful because on the surface he stayed out of the committee problems. He controlled two committees and dominated one. He controlled the majority of the Ways and Means Committee on a crucial item—taxes—in a way that I didn't agree with, especially taxes on oil and gas. He also controlled it in a way I did agree with in regard to trade, but he didn't really control it beyond that. He didn't control the Rules Committee for most of his career. Howard Smith of Virginia was more powerful than Sam Rayburn in the House of Representatives regarding the flow of legislation, and so were some other committee chairmen. Sam Rayburn was for a Tennessee Valley Authority in another part of the country, in the Northwest. It was blocked by a committee chairman who was powerful enough to defy Rayburn and, as a matter of fact, defy his committee and defy the House. So there are all kinds of myths that one needs to get rid of.

Nevertheless, Rayburn was a great legislator. If the Eisenhower people would come to him, or Eisenhower himself would have him down for a drink and a chat, Rayburn would tell them the truth. I've listened to Rayburn on the telephone, saying, "But Ike, you can't do that." So Rayburn was up there telling them what they could and couldn't do, and they'd work things out so that they wouldn't try to do the impossible, unless they wanted to do it for political purposes. You had an entirely different view of what was really going on; Rayburn was getting whipped over and over again. I could tell you some hair-raising anecdotes about how little power he had.

You are, however, absolutely right that the legislative process has been seriously impaired by the increase in subcommittees, and probably by the increase in subcommittee staffs. I'm not sure about the impact of the staff increase, but I am sure that the subcommittees have disintegrated the legislative process. And the reason I'm sure of it is because the only way you could deal with it was through the Rules Committee. You had to be able to have a debate on the floor that was coherent, and the only way you could take four, five or six different committees and make their product coherent, sensible, and fair was by a rule of debate that was very intricate and complicated. If we hadn't been able to do that, the House would have collapsed in a general chaos, and it still could. It very badly needs to be reorganized in terms of committee jurisdictions.

As you probably know, I chaired a committee at the same time we adopted the Budget Act that failed. We got a lot of other interesting things done but not the crucial thing, which was to reorganize the committee system. I am all for modification of the committee system regarding seniority, and I'm all against the subcommittees. I think we need a president to help us on that, by the way, but he [President Reagan] never can say out loud that he is for anything.

QUESTION: Would you care to comment on immigration policies? There seems to be a lack of consensus on the issue.

CONGRESSMAN BOLLING: I have a hard time with the premise that immigrants hurt us because I'm old enough to remember the Irish immigrants and the refugees from middle Europe in the 1940s. I think Hispanic immigrants are doing something for us as well as to us. They are obviously competitive, and they have different religious and cultural attitudes. In the 1940s, Irish-Americans dominated Kansas City politics for years and years. It had happened earlier in the Northeast, in the Boston area, and so on.

I may be foolish, but I think that this country can absorb this diversity. Perhaps the most remarkable thing that we have given the world is our extraordinary ability to absorb diversity. While I don't think it is quite as remarkable as the Constitution and its development, I think the political system is very remarkable. Our ability to absorb variety in a semi-civilized way is very important. I don't think we should turn down people who disagree with us religiously, or in other ways.

QUESTION: But does it fractionalize the country?

CONGRESSMAN BOLLING: I think that is one of the fractionalizations you have to face; that fractionalization is represented in the House. There now is a vast constituency of people who come from another country, and most of the people they elect remain diverse. But the diversity is not creating a whole lot of political divisions, though it is doing so to some degree.

Let me tell you about my successor. He is a black man representing a constituency that is 75 percent white. When I decided to retire, which I did very early, a year before I had to file for the primary, a young black man who had been a legislator, who had come from a black district, decided he would run for Congress. He did so despite the fact that the district was three-quarters white, and if I may say so inelegantly, there are quite a few rednecks in that district.

A lot of people didn't think he had a chance to get nominated. I stayed out of the nominating process because I knew that I wouldn't have anything useful to do if I got myself involved in it early. He got himself nominated and won, although the odds were against him. The skeptics said, "Kansas City is not going to elect him. The people are not ready to elect a black." In any event Alan Wheat got elected and reelected a couple of times, and he is probably going to have a great, not just good, congressional career.

I think this proves something unique. There is maybe one other district in the country—I'm not absolutely sure about it—where a black man represents a majority white constituency. It may be true in Berkeley, California where

Ron Dellums runs, though Ron Dellums and Alan Wheat are very different people. It seems to me that we have something very interesting happening. The people of Kansas City are plain, ordinary American people, largely white, and very heterogeneous. But they have voted for Wheat repeatedly. I don't know how meaningful this is, except that it makes me feel pretty optimistic about the American people and their ability to think about their problems.

When they think about the problems that they have, they may seem very acute. They need to think about the problems America has in the world and its responsibility in the world. It wouldn't do us a bit of harm if we had a better understanding about the religions and cultures of the Far East, the Middle East, and Africa. I myself am guilty of not knowing the African religions and the attitudes associated with them. Suppose we had more people from these backgrounds living in this country? We would learn very quickly what the problems are in the countries they come from, as if we lived with them.

I had an experience today that I thought was absolutely fascinating. We wanted to have a sandwich before we came here. We pulled up at a place which called itself a deli. It was out in the country, and it was a very nice place. It turned out that the proprietor was a man from Iran. He had been a film maker and fled Iran because he had been involved in making a film for the government of the Shah. But the proprietor was defending Iran as being attacked unfairly by Iraq, despite the fact that he had been run out of the country. He would surely have been killed if he'd stayed, but here he was still defending his country, though not his government. I don't think that's a bad thing, to have such a diner sitting on a highway in Virginia.

QUESTION: I am thinking about your Lippmann anecdote and the fact that nobody wants to hear about the House. I wonder if you can allay my fears about the negative attitudes in our culture which have developed toward Congress and specifically the House.

There was a moment last summer during the Iran-Contra hearings when I thought that Brendon Sullivan [Oliver North's lawyer] was saying, in coaching Oliver

North, "The way we can win this thing is to make it a battle of North against Congress; a solitary military hero and patriotic figure against congressional characters, too many of whom are old crocodiles." That played pretty well. To me it showed that the understanding of what this institution is all about wasn't there. Let me formulate it this way: the attitude contained more than boredom or disinterest; it contained a certain animus against Congress. This President can say, "All North did was not tell Congress everything; I do that myself," and get a laugh. There is a lot of negative imagery surrounding Congress, and specifically the House. I feel that it has increased, and there was a moment last summer when the negative image of Congress became very strong. Tell me I'm wrong.

CONGRESSMAN BOLLING: No, I don't think you are wrong. Part of the reason is that Congress very badly needs to reorganize itself, the House in particular. I am not sure about the Senate because I simply don't understand the Senate as well as I do the House. But the House desperately needs to have a reorganization that makes it work somewhat better. I think reorganization is possible with the help of a very well organized set of lobby groups on the outside to assist in convincing individual members of the House of the need to reorganize and with a president who is not hostile.

Some legislation with which I was involved and which would have reorganized the institution very substantially was not a cinch to lose. It didn't get passed because we made a few mistakes, because of bad luck, and, unlike the issue on which the Budget Act rode into being, because it didn't get good press. We had reasonably good support from a variety of places, but we didn't get good press. While I think it is absolutely essential that the Congress do that, I don't think it will happen without a president who is understanding of Congress.

One of the bad breaks that we had on that Select Committee of Committees was that Ford, who helped set up the committee, left the House. Carl Albert consulted with Ford, when he was still in the House, on setting up the Select Committee on Committees. It would have helped us if Ford had been there, and it would have helped institutional reform if he had remained in the presidency because he was friendly. We need a president who understands the House and who is clever enough to be able to convey his sympathy, though he can't afford to go public with it. If he goes public with his support, he automatically creates opposition among representatives who fear that the president is trying to interfere in their districts. That simply isn't so. Jack Kennedy was in on the fight we had in 1961, which gave the power to control the flow of legislation back to the Speaker as opposed to Howard Smith, but he never acknowledged this publicly.

Maybe there's another thing that we ought to talk about on this. A lot of what happens in Congress has to be secret in the preliminary stages. There is no way on earth that you can work out a very difficult political issue unless you do it in secrecy. That does not mean that your acts in a committee or on the floor should not be recorded. Everybody's votes should be known. But when you begin to work on a very difficult problem like the Marshall Plan or the first Civil Rights Act, you have to have secrecy because the people, who represent districts and interest groups, have to have a chance to go back with a plan to consult with at least some of their constituents on what will work. When you get into the process, you have to go completely public. So you need secrecy in the conceptual stage. The best example of that is of course the Constitution. They had to have secrecy initially, or they never could have gotten this document passed that won state by state by very narrow margins. When you are fighting with narrow margins politically, you simply must have the ability to put together your piece without public knowledge. All bipartisan efforts are done that way. Part of the problem then, is that Congress can't defend itself.

QUESTION: I have two questions. One is rather general and the other is more precise. The first one has to do with your view that President Johnson was a failure. I am interested in how you would contrast him with Kennedy. And more specifically, my recollection is that Johnson secured the passage of legislation that Kennedy couldn't get through Congress. Is that correct?

CONGRESSMAN BOLLING: That's right.

QUESTION: I understand your view is that despite Johnson's civil rights legislation and his war on poverty, he was a failure because he disturbed relations with Congress and some of his legislation went too far.

CONGRESSMAN BOLLING: No, each of these presidents was different. Johnson passed all kinds of legislation that Kennedy couldn't get through. You don't have to look very far to see why. Kennedy never had anything like a friendly Congress. Johnson passed very important civil rights laws. I happen to know a great deal about them as I was involved in the details, including when Johnson shifted the priorities from the tax cut first—which was Kennedy's approach—to civil rights. Johnson used the sympathy for Kennedy to do something dramatic about civil rights. It was magnificent. I think Johnson is a great president, as well as a failed president, because of that.

Incidentally, the civil rights legislation had already passed the House under Kennedy. Johnson, however, reversed the Senate by using the power of the office. That deserves a lot of credit. On the other hand, he not only ran over Congress, but also ignored advice from Congress. He'd always taken it when it had come from Rayburn's mouth. Later, there was nobody there that he'd listen to, not a soul. He made excessive demands because he never argued the case for how much should be done later on.

In 1965 when all the great programs that should have come up in 1945 came up in smaller measure, he received an overwhelming majority, which he then misused. We never did achieve anything substantial about the District of Columbia because he overreached himself. He didn't maintain a balanced approach, although some of the things he did were wonderful. Nevertheless, he didn't handle the economy well; he started the inflation. Also, of course, I don't think he dealt very well with the Vietnam situation. But I don't want to make an issue out of that. I just think he overdid it. He pressured congressmen rather than worked with them.

I am trying to say that Congress produces some wisdom as well as some clowns.

QUESTION: It looks like the budget touches right on that subject. Could you give some examples of legislation that, in your opinion, he went too far on? My second question concerns your view of the recent proposal that the president be given a line item veto.

CONGRESSMAN BOLLING: Well, I'm one of the very few Democrats who is basically for the line item veto, and this is why: I think it will take away some of the power committee chairmen shouldn't have, such as getting a number of pet projects passed when they aren't really justified.

I served as chairman of the Rules Committee for a number of years and I had too much power. Nobody should have that much power. In the last six months of a two year term I had more power over legislation than the president. I realize that's an awfully strong statement, but I had life or death power on virtually any piece of legislation unless it had unanimous support. That power of congressmen needs to be curbed. I shall even name such a congressman. Jamie L. Whitten has taken such good care of Mississippi that it is amazing to me that there is anything wrong in Mississippi. I don't think people should be allowed to do what Jamie L. Whitten did, and I think only a line item veto can do it.

This raises a lot of problems of course, and if it goes through, it will go through on a great, big, complicated deal where power is shared in different ways. Perhaps it will go through on a complicated lousy deal, which is related to the legislative veto. I don't know, but that's how things get done in the real world. It may turn up, for all I know, in the modifications of the Budget Act which very badly needs to be modified. I'm not giving you a very optimistic answer. It is going to be a tough piece of work.

Regarding the examples of excessive demands made by Johnson, I think the example of the Office of Economic Opportunity (OEO) is the saddest one, and at the same time the most important bill among those that should have been done moderately. The OEO should have been started out relatively small with a good many of the principles included, but he kept it growing like Social Security. He wanted to get constituency for it and keep it there. I don't pretend to be able to list all these bills without going back and looking them up. Generally speaking, the ones that Nixon knocked out are the ones that went too far, and the ones that survived Nixon's attempts at elimination are the ones that were done right. That's a very pragmatic explanation, but it is fairly accurate. If Nixon couldn't get rid of them, then they were probably pretty well accepted.

In other words, legislation shouldn't be acceptable only in a partisan sense, but it should be sustainable in a broadly-gauged national sense if it is to last. The legislature and the president, in my view, have a responsibility for not putting too much on the table. Johnson's program, if looked at in economic terms was nuts, although I loved all the ideas it contained.

QUESTION: Is a bipartisan foreign policy possible? If so, would you please address U.S. policy toward the Soviet Union in this context?

CONGRESSMAN BOLLING: Yes, we can have a bipartisan foreign policy. This is one of the areas, however, in which I can't be polite about President Reagan. My main criticism of President Reagan is that he doesn't do his job; his job is not to be a cheerleader, but to be the master of our foreign and defense policy and to maintain a society that is stable. For a society to be stable it has to be relatively at peace with itself, which makes necessary all the social legislation I have talked about.

I don't think President Reagan has ever known enough about the realities of foreign policy to be a president. I don't think he has ever tried to know enough. I have been scared to death of his lack of knowledge about the defense establishment. I'm not against the defense establishment as such; I think it is crucial that we have a strong defense. While I have been against some weapons systems, I have supported others. Generally I'm thought of as a hawk, at least by my critics. But I don't think we need to have the kind of military base we have been building. We've been throwing money at the military in a way Johnson threw money at domestic programs. I think that is madness and that we have a real problem.

For years we tried to put together a bipartisan consensus in Congress to reform the defense establishment. It began after I retired in 1981-82. I was fascinated to watch it. Perhaps it was a reaction to what I consider Reagan's excess, compared to the reasonable increase in defense undertaken by Carter. (I mean the first time Carter increased defense spending, not the second time when he seemed to sweeten the pot and perhaps was playing politics as he left the presidency.)

In any event, Senator Sam Nunn and a variety of other people, not all of whom I know very well, are very busy trying to rationalize our defense establishment and defense policy. Behind that, of course, is the need for a rational foreign policy and behind that is the competition with the Soviet Union. My view on the Soviet Union hasn't changed an iota. I have been almost a professional anti-Stalinist, although Stalin has been dead for a long time.

Despite that, I feel that at all times you have to be in communication with the Soviet Union as much as with China. Presently I'm a little bit less of a hard-liner than I was. But I'll probably be more of a hard-liner in the next years for the reason that the American people will be in one of their euphoric phases when they think of the Soviet Union as a friend. I won't be. I think we have to have a balanced defense; I think we have to be careful about our commitments; I think we have a major responsibility in the democratic world. Part of that requires an aggressive effort to get along with the Soviet Union and reduce the piles of weapons for which we really don't have much use. We ought to keep the ones we need.

QUESTION: I wonder what would happen if we had an ideological and stubborn president who could use the line item veto and deny the House the right to override? Wouldn't he be able to destroy months or years of legislation?

CONGRESSMAN BOLLING: That's a very good question. Superficially the answer probably would be that he could. But the fact of the matter is that when you get into these struggles the people who turn out to be ideological fanatics are relatively few in number. Nevertheless, today we are facing for the first time in my experience a significant number of people who have decided that near-fanaticism is the only way in which the Republicans will regain the House. So you have some very bright people, including a man from Georgia named Newt Gingrich, who are very far to the right and insist on being confrontational.

I don't think they are going to succeed. I've met enough Republicans in meetings where we were not conferring as partisans but as people who wanted to get things done. But the last thing we need today is the confrontational approach taken by a few Republican fanatics. What we need with our economic difficulties, which in my opinion are enormous, is civility. Even though we still have a remnant of euphoria about the economy, at least in some parts of the population, I see problems ahead. I hate to use the word that some people think indicates weakness, but "civility" is one of the things that we very badly need in the times ahead.

Let me just have a short discourse on the problem of civility. At this moment we are in the election process. That's the time to fight. If possible, you ought to do it in a way that is educational, but now is the time to do it. When everybody is elected and has become part of the government, that's the time to work together. It isn't very smart to play party electoral politics year-round. You ought to be able to confine your party politics to election time, and regardless of whether you win or lose, be civil about the outcome.

Take those people who did the Constitution. Those people had been at each other's throats on previous occasions. Jefferson and Hamilton, for example, had violently differing views. But they knew they had to work together once the controversy about the Constitution was settled. In the same way we have somehow to get the American people and the Congress to work together, and the president has to learn that first. Then we won't have to worry about the item veto and legislative conflict.

If Harry Truman could get Vandenberg and company who comprised very large numbers in the House and Senate, to consent to a bipartisan foreign policy, why can't anybody else?

NARRATOR: One of the legitimate criticisms of social science and academic work is that so often it is too far removed from the patient in the bed, and doesn't deal with the real issues. Dick Bolling's service in the Eighty-first to the Ninety-sixth Congress amounted to some thirty-four years in which he was very close to the patient in the bed, and he is quite willing to diagnose the condition of the patient. That's why it is so important to have him here today to speak about a very neglected problem in American political history and political practice. We are all extremely grateful to him for coming.

The Living Constitution

DOUGLASS CATER

Douglass Cater was born in Montgomery, Alabama. He began his education at Phillips Exeter Academy and received undergraduate and graduate degrees at Harvard. He embarked on a career in journalism with the *Reporter* magazine, serving first as its Washington editor and later national affairs editor. He has taught at Princeton, Wesleyan, Stanford, and the University of California at San Francisco and directed the Aspen Institute program council and served as senior fellow. He received the George Polk Memorial award and the New York Newspaper Guild First Page award for his writings and journalism. He served in the OSS in World War II. His career in public service began in the early 1950s when he was special assistant to the secretary of the army. He is the author of numerous books including *Ethics in a Business Society* with Marquis Childs, *Dana: The Irrelevant Man*, *The Fourth Branch of Government*, and *Power in Washington*. It is a great pleasure to once again welcome President Douglass Cater of Washington College in Fredericksburg, Maryland to the Miller Center.

MR. CATER: Thank you, Ken. It feels like coming home again. I can't remember how many times I've sat around this table.

I have just finished five years as president of a historic, small college. It has been a challenging period, but this summer I took a semi-sabbatical to think about how much longer I wanted to endure eight day work weeks, spending a great part of my time on my knees—not praying, but begging—which is the fate of the small college president.

In beginning, I would like to note the bicentennial celebration of the longest living written Constitution still in force in the world. The conception of our Constitution in Philadelphia was a miracle, the real birth of America, and we should not in any way minimize the significance of its framing. And yet we do recognize that we are under a *living*, as opposed to a *literal*, constitution. This distinction has attracted attention with the recent ordeal of Judge Bork. He has brought into national prominence the phrase "original intent" and I would like to use that as a recurring theme in this discussion.

Thirty years ago I wrote *The Fourth Branch of Government*, which was one of the first books to recognize the powerful role that the press plays in the scheme of American government. A number of my journalistic friends were offended to have their profession termed a branch of government. They cried, "We are totally independent; we are not beholden to the government and to call us a branch of government is demeaning." I think they overlooked the fact that governing in America is a broadly consuming activity. In fact, many institutions have been called a fourth branch. Lobbyists used to be called the fourth branch. The regulatory agencies were called the fourth branch. It is my opinion that the press is more legitimately a fourth branch than any of these other participants.

Later I wrote *Power in Washington*, which attempted to examine the changes in the organization of power since World War II. It was a coincidence that I arrived in Washington as a young reporter in the very same month that Senator Joseph McCarthy went to Wheeling, West Virginia and made known his list of "communists" who were in his words, "infiltrating the State Department." It was my experience to witness what Henry Adams calls one of those periodic "hiccups" of democracy in which power is disordered for a number of years.

It became clear to me as a back seat driver in the press corps that we were watching a new style demagogy. The old demagogue was the master of the stump speech who played on basic hatreds in a way that gave him a popular appeal. McCarthy, however, was not a very good orator at all. His skill, rather, was in timing the release of information to make claims, assertions, charges, and accusations appear to be objective news. He was doing this just as prime time television news was becoming a regular phenomenon in America. He was quite skillful in manipulating that glimpse on the cave wall (to use a platonic image) which television was providing to the citizenry. And for a remarkable number of years he was able to stage his acts to gain center stage in Washington. Indeed, in the latter years of the Truman administration and the early years of the Eisenhower administration he successfully diverted attention from the larger purposes of these presidents. It was this experience and others in watching government and trying to read my Constitution, not in the way a hard-shell Baptist reads his Bible, but by finding what is the living Constitution, that led to the reflections that were part of *Power in Washington.*

The election of our president dramatically demonstrates how far we have come from what Judge Bork calls "original intent." If we strictly abided by the framers' original intent, about this time, a year or so from a presidential election, this group would possibly be debating over who among us deserved to be our elector. Then, according to the Constitution, we would choose him by whatever method the state legislature had provided. Having chosen our elector, we would not allow him to go to Washington to engage in cabals and factions or to work out some sort of combine to pick the chief magistrate. Instead he would meet in the state capitol with a few of his fellow electors from the state and send to Washington the name of the person he felt most suited to be president. And by amendment of the Constitution, he would also send the name of the person most suited to be vice president. This is the way it was supposed to be, but this is not popular democracy. I don't think the Founding Fathers had the foggiest notion of popular democracy. Yet this system based on "original intent" lasted only two elections. We moved to the national nominating conventions, and then early in this century, to the primaries. Today we are fast moving toward the notion of a national primary.

How far have we come toward the idea of plebiscitary democracy? I saw Jimmy Carter speak at the Gerald Ford Library on the experiment of interactive television. This uses a device for television sets which instantly polls the audience. Carter said words to the effect: "How wonderful it would be if a president could make a speech and the people could respond that same evening to show their support for what he said." I went up to Carter afterwards and asked, "Do you really think that's the way we should govern this republic, by polling every night?" Yet we already have gone a considerable distance toward this under the umbrella of our living Constitution. I am not suggesting that we should take immediate steps to return to the "original intent" of the Founders regarding the electoral college. Yet I must confess that the process at which we have arrived for selecting presidents has become so disorderly that it reminds me of something Groucho Marx once said: "I would not be a member of a club that would elect me as a member." I would not be a president of a nation that put me through the process that one must endure to become a bona fide candidate for president.

I saw Dan Evans of Washington, one of the men whom I really admire in the Senate, when he announced that he was retiring. I later wrote him a letter asking him, "Are you retiring because the political process is no longer providing the kind of satisfactions and encouragements that you expected?" I think we are witnessing in those who are not standing for president significant signs that the business of presidential campaign politics has gotten out of hand.

One of the evidences of divine inspiration at Philadelphia is the "separation of powers". Article I, Section I states, "The legislative power shall be vested in the Congress." There is no mention here of the president, except later on it is suggested that he would have a veto over acts of legislation, subject to two-thirds override by the two chambers.

The living Constitution, since the time of Franklin Roosevelt, makes the president the chief legislator. Now it is Congress which vetoes or modifies what is essentially the president's program and the president's budget. It is not the House that originates revenue measures, but the president. Even when we have a divided government with a Republican president and a Democratic Congress, the Congress blames the president for not presenting a unified, balanced budget. Now there is an effort to create a summit conference between the Congress and the president in order to reduce the budget deficit.

Article II, Section I states "The executive power shall reside in the President." There is no mention in the literal Constitution of congressional committees and subcommittees. Yet under the living Constitution we have what my book calls "subgovernments," or what political scientists have come to call the "iron triangles"—those coalitions from the executive branch, the congressional subcommittees, and the interest groups—which daily make decisions on issues of particular concern to them. It is no longer by any means clear that executive power is confined to the executive branch. Congress has little hesitancy to step into the decision-making process.

The Supreme Court, to everyone's surprise, declared unconstitutional the so-called "legislative veto" by which either chamber of Congress could exercise an *ex post facto* decision on the executive use of power. This Supreme Court ruling went back to original intent. But Congress' daily oversight by the various committee and subcommittee directives continues. The living Constitution is not what the literal Constitution foresaw.

Then there is the "limbo land," the territory that exists somewhere between Congress and the president. The Constitution states quite clearly that Congress shall have the power to declare war and that the Senate shall have the power of advice and consent over treaties. And yet all our wars since World War II have been fought without a declaration of war on the part of Congress. Treaties have been largely replaced by executive agreements.

We confront another murky area with the War Powers Act by which Congress has now attempted to reclaim the power to declare war. Congress wants to be able to come along after sixty days and say, "That's a war and now you have to call the troops home unless you can get us to declare war." Instead of reclaiming its pristine constitutional power, Congress is saying that it wants to get into the act with the president as commander in chief, and in a sense, second guess the conduct of war. Every president since Mr. Nixon, who vetoed it, has declared the War Powers Act unconstitutional. Yet nobody has figured out a way to take the case to the Supreme Court.

Apparently we must get into a war and then go ask the Supreme Court, "Is this Act for real or not?"

Under the Treaty Provision we have the phenomenon of compliance with SALT II despite its never having been considered by the Senate for ratification. So there is again the threat of constitutional confrontation between the two branches which nobody knows how to reconcile. Indeed some in Congress are now proposing a subpoena on the executive to get the SALT II negotiating documents in order to see whether the President is telling the truth about the understandings that related to tests in space. If they do this, Congress will have taken one more giant stride to undermine the executive privilege of confidentiality, which lies at the very heart of presidential decision-making.

I was greatly disconcerted when Mr. Donald Regan appeared before the Iran-Contra Committee. Senator Heflin of Alabama said to him, "I understand you have waived your Fifth Amendment rights," and he said, "Yes, I have." Then Mr. Regan added, "I've also waived executive privilege." Where under the Constitution is a former deputy to a president given any executive privilege that he might wave? Executive privilege is nowhere mentioned in the Constitution. Rather, it has grown up under usage as the right of a president to put a cloak over matters in which he was personally involved. It certainly has not been thought of as a right which a presidential appointee could claim. I wrote an article in *The Washington Post* on this matter and Mr. Regan's lawyers got very angry with me.

Finally, we have Article III, Section I which states, "Judicial power shall reside in the Supreme Court and such lesser courts as shall be appointed." In *Brown vs. the Board of Education*, the Supreme Court was years ahead of Congress and the president in declaring as fundamental law that separate cannot be equal under the Constitution. An "activist" Supreme Court not only interpreted constitutionality, but also set a new dimension of equality under the law. Yet the same Supreme Court appears to avoid like the very devil any attempt to adjudicate the power confrontations between the other two branches of government. Harry Truman's seizure of the steel mills provoked one such case, and more recently the Supreme Court decision on legislative vetoes.

I am suggesting, then, that the disorder of power in Washington today relates to two areas nowhere mentioned in the Constitution and therefore very difficult to resolve through judicial or other means. One area is entitled executive privilege: both Watergate and Irangate led to dramatic erosion of executive privilege. The president, in a sustained competition for the support of public opinion, will find it very, very difficult to claim, "This is a matter too confidential for me to reveal to the Congress." Yet anyone who has worked in the White House and realizes the confidentiality required if there is to be free debate during difficult decision-making, can foresee that it is going to be very difficult for any president, no matter how well motivated, to do his job without this confidentiality.

The other area of controversy relates to congressional "oversight," another word that is not mentioned in the Constitution. Thomas Jefferson did talk of "the grand inquest" of Congress as a method by which Congress could keep the executive at bay. Congressional oversight today more often than not has no legislative purpose in mind. Rather it is designed to give maximum publicity to Congress in the restraints on executive power. Legislative oversight, when performed well and wisely, provides one of our system's checks and balances. When it is carried to the point that Congress pulls up the plant of policy-making before it is well rooted, it can do fundamental damage. It creates a compulsion on the president and his minions to come up with quickie solutions merely to stay one jump ahead in the decision-making process.

Richard Neustadt, in his celebrated book *Presidential Power: The Politics of Leadership*, claims that we really don't have separation of powers under our Constitution; rather we have separated institutions sharing powers. The living Constitution bears him out. It was with this understanding that I looked at the fourth branch of government, the press. Because our institutions are separate, not one of them—neither the executive nor the legislative nor the judicial branch—is prepared to concede to another the principal role in the communication process. This promotes the unelected functionary, the journalist, who comes to Washington, frequently with no more than a paycheck from his publisher, to an important *de facto* role.

109

He is the principal means of the daily communication of government. Not only is he communicating to the larger public beyond Washington, but he is more likely than not the one who first carries the news between the opposite ends of Pennsylvania Avenue. His priority in mediating the flow of news about government constitutes the real power of the press, far more so than any purely editorial power.

I was satisfied at the time I wrote *The Fourth Branch of Government* that I had made a significant discovery. Indeed after traveling around the world on a fellowship and comparing the way government related to the press in Britain, the Soviet Union, Germany, and India, I was more convinced than ever that in the American system of separated institutions, the press plays a peculiarly significant role.

What has changed in the thirty years since I wrote that book? When I wrote, television was just intruding its nose into the door. I remember how angry we print journalists were when Jim Hagerty [press secretary for President Eisenhower] permitted television cameras to come into the president's press conference. If you remember, he made them hold their films for a couple of hours in his early years. Print journalists were given a two hour head start.

Then came John Kennedy, for whom television was created. He was the first of the video personalities. He had the gestures and the manner that suited television. Live television coverage of the press conference plus behind-the-scenes television coverage of a good many things going on in the Kennedy White House became the norm.

Today we have a President who is trying his best to figure out how to use television without having to deal with television reporters. We are reconciled to seeing Mr. Reagan on television as he gets on or off of a helicopter. He has abolished the president's press conference as a regular mode of communication. Yet he has been what we feared when television was first invented: a showman turned into a consummate politician. His manner of delivery obliges you to like him even when you hate what he has to say.

Yet it looks as if Reagan is going to meet the same fate of every president since Truman, with the exception of

110

Eisenhower. Every one of these men, before departing the White House, has been severely crippled by the experience of being president. One paradox is that in the age termed the "imperial presidency," we have witnessed a succession of presidents diminished by the exercise of power. I foresee the same fate for Mr. Reagan. I think he is on the slippery, downward slope in which one damn thing after another hits him. Once again the public is waiting for a new kind of leader to emerge. I find an awful lot to worry about in the age of electronic communication. The ideal, of course, would be that the television set would turn America into a great Greek marketplace where citizens gather before their living room sets and participate in the open forum of democracy. The reality is that we have developed a new breed of public opinion manipulators who surround each candidate for president.

When Walter Mondale attempted to run in the mid-1970s, he came out to San Francisco when I was teaching at the University of California. I went to a dinner for him and as he spoke to a gathering to begin the fund-raising process, I thought to myself, this man looks as if he has already lost heart. A month or so later he announced that he had withdrawn from the competition. People remember that he said that he was tired of living in Holiday Inns. But they forget that he also said: "I'm tired of arriving in communities at 6:00 in the evening and having to sum up my views on some weighty matter of foreign policy in thirty seconds or less for the evening news." This, of course, is what the candidate is expected to do, over and over again. If he slips and repeats himself, or even worse, if he slips and repeats somebody else, he is consigned to ignominy. As Senator Biden declared, "Let he who is without sin cast the first stone." The age of instant communication is creating an environment in which the conduct of farsighted politics is very, very difficult.

Recently, I managed to persuade Pete DuPont, who is running for president, to give me four dates for a debate at Washington College. He was willing to debate any Democrat. Then I began to go after the Democrats. I couldn't get yes, I couldn't get no, and I couldn't even get a maybe out of them. They were all so fixated on Iowa and what will play in Iowa that the notion of speaking in

111

Delaware, or Maryland, was beyond their capacity, and more importantly, the capacity of those cunning manipulators who surround them. One is figuring out how to manipulate public opinion polls, another is figuring out how to create television imagery, and another one of them is handling press relations. These people are the presidential candidate's coterie. He does not communicate with other politicians. It is a lonely game nowadays and it is loners who are elected president, like Carter and like Reagan. They are men who don't have a circle of eminent friends with whom they engage in discussion. It was said of Johnson, by George Reedy, that his great downfall began when he withdrew from the hugger-mugger of the Senate. "Where," Reedy said so eloquently, "he was used to being told 'go soak your head'."

This is a brief enumeration of what I consider the disorders of power. I do not believe that television has an ideological bias. I don't think that it's out to get Reagan or to get somebody else. If it has any mission, it is exploitive. Television journalists seek to expose the soft underbelly of public policy, the merry ride of the business of governing. Those who succeed in television journalism, unlike some of those who set the peer group attitudes when I entered print journalism, fail to understand what the business of governing is all about. Even if a good governor were to turn up in the White House, I don't think the television journalists would have the capacity to differentiate him from less capable predecessors.

With this comes the continuing conviction, spawned by television, that the citizen should be the instant arbiter of every controversial issue that confronts government, no matter how complicated it may be and no matter how long term its solution. Television is the ultimate appeal to the people. It recalls the word popular in the days of the Founding Fathers, "ochlocracy," or demagogy of the masses. The Founders feared this demagogy just as they feared factions.

Recently I attended a breakfast at which Governor Schaefer of Maryland honored Tom Peters, author of *In Search of Excellence*. Peters has written a new book, dedicated to Governor Schaefer, whom he calls the mayor of Maryland because he is trying to run the state the way he ran the city of Baltimore. The title of his book is significant for our time. It is called *Thriving on Chaos*, which Peters defines as the new mode of leadership. Peters did not simply mean thriving *amid* chaos, but actually thriving *on* chaos. So perhaps this is the new polity that is evolving, a system of governing that does thrive on chaos. I have yet to be convinced how it is going to work. I guess I am an "original intent" man on this point, although I would not have voted for Judge Bork.

QUESTION: You've seen the chaos that I've seen for a lifetime in Washington. Do you think that a line item veto, giving an executive authority to manage the affairs of government, will ever come about?

MR. CATER: Lloyd Cutler wrote an article in *Foreign Affairs* several years ago called "To Form a Government." After reflecting upon his years in the Carter White House, he stated that the principal problem of American government is that when we elect a president, we do not form a government. He was strongly influenced by his experience with the British parliamentary system. Drawing on that article, he managed to gather associates, including Doug Dillon and Kansas Senator Nancy Kassebaum as co-chairmen, into a "Committee on the Constitution." I was a member, and we spent four years meeting every three or four months, usually for a day or sometimes for a day and a half, to consider possible amendments to the Constitution or other organic changes in governing. I must admit that we came up with precious few proposals for which we could get support, including the line item veto.

I have mixed feelings about the line item veto. If we had given that power to Reagan, we know what he would have done with it. We would have had the military budgets he wanted and the civilian budgets he wanted. I guess that's my dilemma; while I want a strong and purposeful president, I also want the president to be somebody whom I believe in. That may be a contradiction.

We examined other proposals like the six year term for the presidency. Just as we were fully getting into that, Irangate came along and our momentum seemed to peter out. Nobody was pushing the six year presidency very hard. We did reach a consensus that four year terms for the representatives would be valuable. There were several senators on this committee, however, and they said that the congressmen would have to pledge that in their off year they would not run against the senator in their state. Otherwise the Senate would not ratify this amendment to the Constitution. The senators, of course, feel that they should serve for life, and more and more congressmen are beginning to feel this way. Elective turnover in the House of Representatives today is small. They leave either when they get weary and sick or else, as Tip O'Neill found out, when they realize that they can earn money on their pensions.

We decided in the end that this modest ambition for a four year House term would not cut the mustard as an amendment to the Constitution. President Johnson, you may remember, in his State of the Union address, proposed a four year term. He got a standing ovation in the House. Then they never even brought the bill up for consideration.

QUESTION: I'd like to hear your remedy for the process of selecting presidential nominees. Obviously it is too expensive, grueling and bizarre. Have you thought of a remedy for this?

MR. CATER: The remedy lies not in abolishing primaries, because I think that they are too sacred to us, but rather in reform of the primaries. This would probably not require any constitutional change. It could be done by the party leadership. I advocate regional primaries. They would start rather late, say March of the year in which the election was to be held. They would take place at scheduled intervals so that the candidates would have time to go from one to the other. Also, as part of the general reform, the national nominating conventions would be heavily weighted toward those members of that party who hold elective or appointive office. Only a minority of delegates should come from the activists who provide instant enthusiasm for one candidate or another. These are the summer soldiers, the ones who are ready to work twenty-four hours a day as long as they are pushing George McGovern, but who fade back into the woodwork when somebody else comes along.

114

These are not the kind of supporters who build enduring parties. So I would tilt the convention toward the more professional politicians and away from the amateurs.

Having done that, I would try to give respectability to the presidential debates. I have worked very closely with the League of Women Voters in trying to make the debates more worthwhile. At the present the League is a pawn. The candidates' managers treat the League with loathing, as do the networks. They think the League is nothing but meddling women who have gotten into the middle of the political process. Either the League or some nonpolitical, nonmedia group should stage the debates and at least four of them should be held in the final campaign. I would think that they should be held in Constitution Hall to remind people that we have a long heritage in this country. The debates represent one of the few opportunities we have to see a candidate living by his own wits. Most of the time when we see him he is programmed by his staff.

The debates are not the greatest thing ever invented, but they are better than anything else. They provide that element of personal conflict which the public demands. The viewership of the debates proves that at least the public will watch them, whereas a great many other political events are ignored. I think involvement in politics is a losing game at the moment. Despite all the efforts of television, the great American public is more apathetic toward the political process today than it was before the age of television.

QUESTION: What about campaign spending?

MR. CATER: I think that the Supreme Court acted correctly when it upheld limits on the amount that a citizen can give to an individual candidate. Still, there are no limits to the amount a candidate can give himself, and he may happen to be a very wealthy person. Nor are there limits to the amount that citizens can give to political action committees. As a result, we have seen the proliferation of political action committees which have the freedom to advertise a candidate on their own terms. And the candidate, since he has no control over their money, has no way to say, "No, that's not the real me they are talking about." I think that this constitutional right of the political action committees to raise and spend their money without any kind of check is a threat to candidates and to the public. So yes, I would say that we should strengthen the present presidential campaign financing act and make it apply to all money that goes into presidential politics. Indeed, I would extend these restrictions to congressional campaigns.

The influence of money on congressional politics, however, begins in the primary system, and there is obviously no way you can put a governmental subsidy into the congressional primary process. So all you can do is reconcile yourself to the fact that money will continue to play a very significant role in the way we elect our people to Congress. Remember that the amendment to the Constitution which declared that senators would be elected by popular vote rather than appointed by their state legislatures was enacted because the Senate had become a haven for millionaires. We are back to that all over again. The Senate is once again a place for rich people.

QUESTION: Lately I've been reading many kind words about the old party bosses. Is this a proper reaction to today's ailments? What about the quality of candidates under the "boss system?"

MR. CATER: The "good old days" weren't totally good, of course, but when the political bosses operated at their best, they did measure the quality of the candidates. We would never be able, in today's open democracy, to go all the way back to the political bossism of the old times. Yet if we had responsible people of authority in the political parties, able to get together as reasoning people in the back rooms, to finger the person they felt had the best prospect of winning the presidency, I happen to think that we would have improved upon the present method.

You will remember that it was Dick Daley who chose both Adlai Stevenson and Paul Douglas as creatures of a political boss. Some pretty good people emerged under the old "back room system." But I'm not for going all the way back to the back rooms, just part way. By and large I labor under the romantic illusion that the man or woman

116

who doesn't go around lusting for the presidency, conspicuously at least, is more likely to be a good president than the one who somehow thinks, "By God, I'm the best candidate possible."

QUESTION: To return to the issue of the press, how often do you think presidential press conferences should be held?

MR. CATER: At least every two weeks. Eisenhower had one, rain or shine, once a week. Roosevelt had them much more frequently. He just called in the press whenever he felt like it. It was not a very formal thing. Eisenhower, though, was almost religious about it; no matter what was going on, he held his press conference; Truman had the same habit. Those were good times. We could ask any question that we wanted—I was a regular—and the president usually answered. But the president, in those days, felt capable of just saying, "No comment." This was a legitimate answer to any question. If he didn't want to answer a question, he didn't have to.

As long as the president is not directly answerable to Congress, as in a parliamentary system, the press conference is the best way we know to get in there and be sure he is still alive and capable of forming coherent sentences. If it's held periodically, I think the press conference can be a very useful way for a president to communicate with the people. I guess we all harbor illusions, but I really believe that if I were president—and mind you I'm not lusting for the job—I could handle a presidential press conference. I think I would know when to say, "Shucks, fellows, I'll have to look it up; I just don't have the answer to that question today."

COMMENT: I don't think Dan Rather would let you get away with that.

MR. CATER: Dan can't beat me up too hard, because there is a certain respect that is accorded the president by the people. The press is presently somewhat nervous about that tradition. I've had three reporters call me in the last month who were doing feature stories on whether the press has gone too far. So it has become a topic of controversy.

It is a curious change. When I was a reporter we were the down-at-the-heel boys who did a fair amount of leg work and were accustomed to saying "sir" to politicians. We didn't kowtow to them, but at the same time a politician was slightly higher up. If we were invited to their home for dinner, we thought it was pretty nice. Nowadays, a television anchor person in Washington wears far better clothes; he has his tailor, and his coiffeur creator. Now *he* gives the dinner parties to which *politicians* hanker for invites. It has been a real turnaround in the social pecking order between the so-called stars of communication and the poor politicians.

QUESTION: I wonder if the public would be better served if the format of the press conference were changed to that of *Meet the Press*? That is, you rotate ABC, CBS, NBC, Associated Press, and United Press International reporters, so that the few who were selected could ask more questions than presently. It seems to me that even with the great group of reporters, the questions are all very superficial because there is no followup.

MR. CATER: Well, today's reporters have a great skill, which we didn't use as much in my day, of announcing, when they ask their first question, that they have a followup. But, yes, a more in-depth format would be nice. There is, by the way, a certain understanding that the front bench boys and girls are going to ask the questions and the folks in the back of the room will be infrequently and randomly selected to ask a question. I don't know why the President plays this game; I would think sometimes he would get so mad that he would do nothing but call on foreigners in the back of the room, but he doesn't. Every time there is a press conference, it's the so-called "deans of the press corps" who get called on first, including those representing the wire services.

To close, I would like to reflect upon "original intent," constitutional flexibility and change. Recall that the framers of the Constitution, rejecting the Articles of Confederation, locked themselves in a closed room without air conditioning over a hot Philadelphia summer, and under strictest admonitions from George Washington, didn't let a single leak out of that room until they had finished their document. Suppose we feel two hundred years later that we need to get out the pencil and draft anew. How in the hell would we do it? How could we hold a closed session in Philadelphia or anywhere else? Television would be saying that every amendment to the Constitution was being violated. In a sense, then, I'm saying, "You can't get there from here."

NARRATOR: It's been a real privilege to have Doug Cater with us. I have a sense we'll be revisiting his latest new book one of these days at the Miller Center for he continues to ask the fundamental questions about politics and the Constitution.

Concluding Observations

Constitutionalism is the bedrock of the American political system. It may be the great political and social invention of all times. It encompasses all the enduring political ideas that Americans cherish: consent of the governed, separation of powers and the rule of law in an ever changing political context.

Yet for many constitutionalism is an abstraction. It seldom electrifies a crowd as do appeals to liberty or justice. There is something remote about constitutionalism. It lacks the concreteness and immediacy of the goals and ideas that historically have been the rallying cries of campaigns and conventions.

The central purpose of this small volume is to offer the reflections of some very thoughtful observers on the more concrete expressions of constitutionalism. These include a ratification debate on the Constitution and Jefferson's idea of liberty. Even the more philosophical pieces, for example, on constitutionalism and democracy, share the quality of concreteness.

The underlying hope of the authors and editors is that such discourse and analysis will inspire Americans and friends abroad to read more about constitutionalism in the years of the American bicentennial and renew their commitments to its principles.